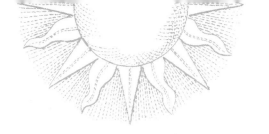

THE GREAT
HISPANIC HERITAGE

Cesar Chavez

THE GREAT HISPANIC HERITAGE

THE GREAT
HISPANIC HERITAGE

Cesar Chavez

Hal Marcovitz

CHELSEA HOUSE
PUBLISHERS

A Haights Cross Communications Company

Philadelphia

CHELSEA HOUSE PUBLISHERS

VP, NEW PRODUCT DEVELOPMENT Sally Cheney
DIRECTOR OF PRODUCTION Kim Shinners
CREATIVE MANAGER Takeshi Takahashi
MANUFACTURING MANAGER Diann Grasse

Staff for CESAR CHAVEZ

ASSISTANT EDITOR Kate Sullivan
PRODUCTION EDITOR Jaimie Winkler
PHOTO EDITOR Sarah Bloom
SERIES & COVER DESIGNER Terry Mallon
LAYOUT 21st Century Publishing and Communications, Inc.

A Haights Cross Communications ✦ Company

http://www.chelseahouse.com

First Printing

1 3 5 7 9 8 6 4 2

Library of Congress Cataloging-in-Publication Data

Marcovitz, Hal.
    Cesar Chavez / Hal Marcovitz.
        p. cm. — (The great Hispanic heritage)
Includes index.
Summary: A biography of the union activist who led the struggle of migrant farm workers for better working conditions.
    ISBN 0-7910-7253-3
    1. Chavez, Cesar, 1927– —Juvenile literature. 2. Labor leaders—United States—Biography—Juvenile literature. 3. Mexican Americans—Biography—Juvenile literature. 4. Mexican American agricultural laborers—History—Juvenile literature. 5. Agricultural laborers—Labor unions—United States—History—Juvenile literature. 6. United Farm Workers—History—Juvenile literature. [1. Chavez, Cesar, 1927– 2. Labor leaders. 3 Mexican Americans—Biography. 4. Migrant labor. 5. United Farm Workers.] I. Title. II. Series.
HD6509.C48 M37 2002
331.88'13'092—dc21

                                                            2002151994

Table of Contents

1

La Huelga

Luis Valdez had been helping to organize a union for migrant farm workers for two years. As head of the theatrical troupe known as *Teatro Campesino* (Farm Workers Theater), Valdez and his cast members lived on the road, driving up and down the coast of California. By performing humorous and satirical plays, the troupe helped spread the message to the poor and mostly illiterate Mexican Americans that the only way they could escape from their lives of poverty and despair was to organize into a labor union and fight together for higher wages and better working conditions.

Certainly, Valdez was used to spending nights in cheap motels along California's rural highways or in crowded inner city apartments lent to the troupe by supporters in the big city *barrios* (neighborhoods). But nothing prepared Valdez for the accommodations he found when the troupe arrived in Borrego Springs, where National Farm Workers of America (NFWA) leader Cesar Chavez had summoned him.

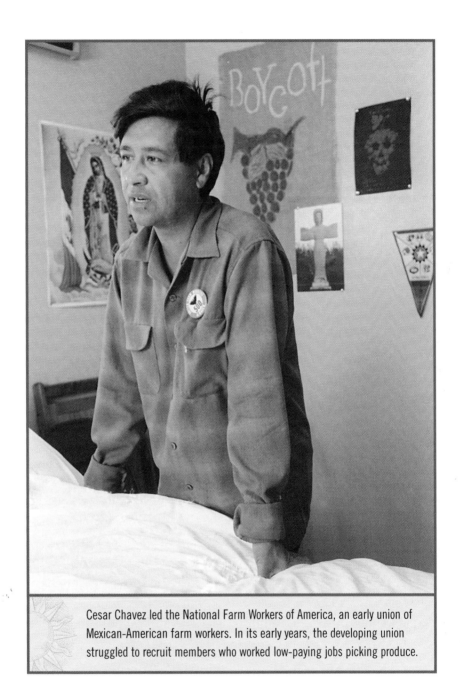

Cesar Chavez led the National Farm Workers of America, an early union of Mexican-American farm workers. In its early years, the developing union struggled to recruit members who worked low-paying jobs picking produce.

Just north of the Mexican border in southern California, Borrego Springs was home to a sprawling grape farm owned by the DiGiorgio Fruit Corporation, one of the largest fruit and vegetable growers in the United States. In September 1965,

Chavez and the NFWA had declared *La Huelga*—the strike—against California growers. When a union declares a strike, the walkout often has an immediate and devastating impact on the industry or the particular business targeted by the job action. With no workers to operate the equipment on the factory floor, production grinds to a halt and the company faces the likelihood of going out of business unless it can find a way to restart. So company officials usually agree to sit down with union leaders to settle their differences by writing a contract, an agreement that sets wages and benefits at a guaranteed level for a guaranteed period of time.

However, during the mid-1960s, the NFWA held no such power over California growers. The union was just beginning to win the confidence of farm laborers and, therefore, had few members. Indeed, Valdez had been summoned to Borrego Springs to help Chavez recruit grape pickers from the DiGiorgio farm fields into the union so they could be asked to join the strike.

Even though migrant farm workers in the mid-1960s worked long days in the sweltering heat for modest wages—sometimes as low as a dollar an hour—union organizers had great difficulty convincing people to walk off their jobs. The workers had no skills, little education and few ways to feed their families beyond picking grapes, lettuce, strawberries and other crops in the farm fields of California and its neighboring states.

Valdez's troupe arrived in Borrego Springs on the night of June 29, 1966. Four days earlier, workers at another DiGiorgio farm near Delano, California, voted to join a union, but not the NFWA. Instead, the workers elected to be represented by the Teamsters, a rough-and-tumble group whose leaders were notorious for their ties to organized crime. Chavez was convinced that the DiGiorgio executives called in the competing Teamsters Union to organize the farm workers, knowing that they could strike quick contracts with the Teamsters, who would agree to terms the NFWA would never accept. Chavez was also convinced

The substandard housing farm owners provided for their workers (like the one pictured here) lacked many common comforts, such as running water. Nevertheless, the National Farm Workers of America still found it difficult to convince their fellow farm workers to risk losing what little they had and join in their peaceful strike efforts.

that the election at the Delano farm was rigged to favor the Teamsters. In fact, during the balloting in Delano, Chavez and other farm workers picketed outside the polling places, admonishing workers not to cast ballots. They shouted, "Don't vote! Don't vote! *Huelga! Huelga!*"

Chavez was determined that the Teamsters would not

stuff the ballot boxes in Borrego Springs. He aimed to send a message to the Mexican Americans that the Teamsters did not have their best interests at heart. He hoped Valdez and the other *Teatro Campesino* members would find ways to appeal to the Mexican-American field workers and draw them away from the Teamsters, who had dispatched tough-talking, white union organizers from Cleveland, Ohio, and other industrial cities to circulate among the farm workers.

When *Teatro Campesino* arrived in town, Valdez drove along the dusty streets searching for the union headquarters.

"We couldn't find the *huelga* headquarters because there was no *huelga* headquarters," Valdez said. "They were staying out at a state a park, where I could see these bundles — *bultos* — these

THE TEAMSTERS

For many years, the Teamsters Union was plagued by corruption at its highest levels. Indeed, from 1957 through 1983, five presidents of the Teamsters were indicted on criminal charges. The most notorious was James R. "Jimmy" Hoffa, who went to jail and later disappeared after his release from prison. Hoffa is presumed to have been murdered. His killers have never been brought to justice.

A reason for much of the corruption in the union is the enormous size of its pension fund. During the 1950s and 1960s, millions of dollars in union pension money was funneled into enterprises backed by organized crime figures, including casinos in Las Vegas, Nevada.

Officially known as the International Brotherhood of Teamsters, Chauffeurs, Warehousemen, and Helpers of America, the union was founded in 1903 and grew into a labor organization representing more than 1.7 million members.

In recent years, leaders pledging to reform the union have assumed power. James P. Hoffa, the son of Jimmy Hoffa, has led them since winning the presidency in 1998.

mounds in the desert. There were men sleeping there. So we got our sleeping bags and proceeded to go out there, and I bumped into somebody. And Cesar rolled over and said, 'OK, you can just lie down here.' He was one of these bunches of people sleeping in the desert sand."

Valdez awoke the next morning to find Chavez had already left the desert camp to establish a picket line outside the DiGiorgio farm. Valdez soon joined his friend on the picket line.

That morning, the NFWA found some measure of success when the union organizers convinced 10 DiGiorgio workers to walk off their jobs and join *La Huelga*. But the migrants had left their clothes and other meager possessions back in the bunkhouses on the farm property. They asked Chavez to accompany them onto the DiGiorgio property to help retrieve their belongings.

Chavez agreed to drive the men onto the DiGiorgio property in his old, dust-caked station wagon. In addition to Chavez, two religious leaders accompanied the migrant workers that day. They were the Reverend Wayne Hartmire, head of the Los Angeles-based California Migrant Ministry, an interdenominational group of church leaders dedicated to helping the migrants, and the Reverend Victor Salandini, a Catholic priest. The 13 men squeezed into the station wagon with Hartmire at the wheel and headed for the DiGiorgio entrance.

They were stopped just inside the gate by a half-dozen nervous DiGiorgio security guards who pointed guns at the car and ordered the men out of the vehicle. Chavez explained to the guards that the men wanted to retrieve their belongings at the DiGiorgio labor camp. But the guards refused to listen to Chavez and ordered the men to climb into the back of a DiGiorgio truck. They were locked inside at gunpoint.

Chavez and the others spent all day locked in the back of the truck. There were just tiny slits in the cargo bay, which let in little light and fresh air. Outside the DiGiorgio farm gates,

Strikers with the National Farm Workers of America carry signs of protest and try to persuade grape pickers to walk off their jobs and join the fight for better conditions in 1965. Although the majority of workers went on strike, the farm businesses survived, operating with a fraction of their normal workforce.

Valdez and other union activists started a loud demonstration, demanding the release of the men. Fearing that a riot could break out at the camp, DiGiorgio executives notified the sheriff's office in nearby San Diego, and at about 10 P.M., a group of deputies arrived to take custody of the 13 men. They were taken from the truck's cargo hold, handcuffed, shackled at the ankles, and placed into a patrol wagon.

Chavez said later that he was delighted to have been arrested. He felt it was important for union leaders to use nonviolent civil disobedience to attain their goals. Chavez was an admirer of Mohandas Gandhi, the Hindu leader who had often been arrested during nonviolent protest while pursuing India's independence from British control. Indeed, on the walls of his small home in Delano, Chavez hung posters of Gandhi as well as the Reverend Martin Luther King, Jr., who also believed in nonviolent protest to achieve equality for African Americans.

Hartmire also saw the benefits that the arrests would have for the union's cause. The minister said that Chavez "was, of course, not overlooking the strategic importance of such a confrontation."

Still, after spending the previous night sleeping in the desert and all day in the sweltering cargo bay of a truck, Chavez was grateful for the "comfort" he found in the back seat of a patrol wagon.

"In the back seat I fell asleep right away," he said. "Although I was happy because of the confrontation, I was disgusted with the so-called justice we were getting. When I woke up, we were in San Diego. There were all kinds of bright lights in my face and a TV camera poking through the window taking my picture."

Chavez and the other 12 men spent the night in the city jail. The next morning they were charged with trespassing and released on bail. Later, they would be sentenced to three years of probation, meaning they were not required to serve additional jail time.

Nevertheless, the arrests helped the union's cause. Hundreds of migrant workers at Borrego Springs, as well as Delano and other DiGiorgio farms, enraged that Chavez and the others would be arrested and hauled off to jail simply for helping the migrants retrieve their possessions, flocked to the union's recruiters and offered to join *La Huelga*. Meanwhile, state investigators looking into the Delano vote

The principles of Martin Luther King, Jr. (pictured here) and other non-violent leaders inspired Chavez to lead the union in peaceful protest. When Chavez was arrested for helping strikers retrieve their belongings from the farm where they worked, many migrant workers were motivated to join Chavez.

concluded that the union election had been rigged. They recommended a new election. For the first time since its humble beginnings, it appeared as though the National Farm Workers Association was on its way to organizing the migrant workers and forcing DiGiorgio and the other growers to the bargaining table.

"All we need is the recognition of our right to full and equal coverage under every law which protects every other working man and woman in this country," Chavez said. "What we demand is very simple: we demand equality. We do not want or need special treatment unless you abandon the idea that we are equal men."

Rising Star of the CSO

Arizona's countryside is more than just rocky mesas and heat-scorched deserts dotted with prickly cacti and twisted Joshua trees. Indeed, there is fertile farmland in Arizona, particularly in the Gila River Valley near the city of Yuma. The richness of the land is due mostly to the Gila and Colorado rivers, which over the centuries deposited silt and minerals in the valley whenever they flooded. Starting in the early 1900s, the Arizona government erected dams and other irrigation projects to help bring water to farmers in the valley.

Unfortunately, even with the best soil and irrigation, crops often fail. That is what happened on the farm owned by Cesar's father, Librado Chavez. Librado's father, Cesario, established the farm in 1909, three years before Arizona was admitted to the Union. But in 1937, when the crops failed and Librado Chavez could not pay his taxes, the family's Gila River Valley property was put on the auction block and the Chavezes were forced off the land.

Migrant workers, living a nomadic existence and following work, often slept in the desert between jobs or while on strike. The transient lifestyle of these workers made it difficult for them to unionize.

Years later, Cesar Chavez recalled his most vivid memory from the day his family lost their farm: a bulldozer knocking down his home.

"When we were pushed off our land all we could take with us was what we could jam into the old Studebaker or pile on its roof and fenders, mostly clothes and bedding," said Chavez, the second-oldest of Librado and Juana Chavez's five children. "I realized something was happening because my mother was crying, but I didn't realize the import of it at the time. When we left the farm, our whole life was upset—turned upside down. We have been part of a very stable community, and we were about to become migratory workers."

Cesar was 10 years old when his family was forced to leave Arizona. The Chavezes drove west to California where farming was an industry. The Chavezes and their neighbors in Yuma had been family farmers, tilling a few dozen acres by the sweat of their own labor. Many farms in California were owned by gigantic food corporations and sprawled over thousands of acres. They were constantly in need of cheap labor to harvest crops of grapes, lettuce and other produce.

In 1937, America was still suffering through the Great Depression. The Chavez family were not the only displaced workers seeking employment in the California farm fields. By the time the Chavez family's Studebaker headed west, there were already thousands of migrants who fled the poverty of their hometowns in search of work.

"Those early days when we first came to California were really rough," Chavez recalled. He continued:

We were really green, and whenever a labor contractor told us something, we fell for it hook, line and sinker. We didn't know the ropes yet and got hooked every time. I remember the first year we ended up in the fall picking wine grapes for a con- tractor near Fresno. They were bad grapes, there were very few bunches on the vines, and we were the only family working in the field. But we were too green to wonder why we were the only ones, you see. After the first week of work, my father asked the contractor for his pay. 'I can't pay you because I haven't been paid by the winery,' the contractor told my father. But we were broke, absolutely broke, with nothing to eat, so the contractor finally gave us $20 and said we'd get a big check when the winery paid him. We worked for seven weeks like that, and each payday the contractor said he couldn't pay us because the winery hadn't paid him yet. At the end of the seventh week, we went to the contractor's house and it was empty. He owed us for seven weeks' pay and we haven't seen him to this day.

Most other migrant families found similar working conditions. Clearly, the labor system on California farms was designed for the benefit of the growers and the contractors they often hired to supply their farms with labor. Workers were often abused.

Hispanic families also had to face racist attitudes. Just as African Americans in the South were prohibited from attending whites-only schools, eating in whites-only restaurants and shopping in whites-only stores, Hispanics found similar prejudice in 1930s California. At any time, Mexican-American citizens were likely to be stopped by a police officer demanding to see identification. Police were constantly on the lookout for illegal immigrants who slipped across the border from Mexico to find work in America.

During this period, the Chavez family lived in a series of migrant labor camps. Most of these camps were composed of no more than shacks. They were unsanitary and often offered little shelter against the elements. As for education, the children of migrant workers could count on virtually no formal schooling. As soon as their families arrived at a camp to find work, they would enroll their children in the local school. But once the crop was harvested, there was no reason to stay. The family would pack up and look for work elsewhere, which meant pulling the children out of school and enrolling them in a new school somewhere else. By the time Chavez quit school in the eighth grade, he had attended no fewer than 60 schools.

For the next two years, Chavez followed the crops on his own. He was growing into adulthood, and he started developing his own ideas and attitudes. It was during this period that he met his future wife, Helen Fabela, and developed the abrasive attitude and resilience that would plague growers in years to come. While sitting in a movie theater in Delano, Chavez and Helen were told they had taken seats on the whites-only side and would have to move to the Mexican side. Chavez refused. The police were called. Chavez was arrested

A young Chavez holds his diploma after his eighth grade gradua-
tion in 1942. By eighth grade, Chavez's family traveled so much
that he had attended more than 60 schools. After completing
eighth grade, Chavez decided not to continue his education,
opting instead to become a full-time farm worker.

and taken to the Delano Police Station where he had to endure a lecture on the importance of observing Delano's racist segregation laws from the desk sergeant.

In 1944, with World War II nearly over, Chavez joined the U.S. Navy. He was 18 years old. Later, he explained that his enlistment was intended as a means to escape the drudgery of farm labor work. He said, "I was doing sugar-beet thinning, the worst backbreaking job, and I remember telling my father, 'Dad, I've had it!' Neither my mother or father wanted me to go, but I joined up anyway."

If Chavez expected to learn a trade or perform duties of importance for the war effort, he was mistaken. Moreover, he found the same racism in the navy that he experienced at home. After completing training camp, Chavez was shipped to the Mariana Islands in the Pacific Ocean where he spent the last few months of World War II on a paint crew.

His enlistment over in 1946, Chavez returned to Delano. He married Helen in 1948. Eventually, the couple would have eight children.

Their first home was a shack in a labor camp. Chavez worked in the fields, picking grapes and cotton. A year later they moved to San Jose to join Cesar's brother, Richard, who found steady employment on an apricot farm. Cesar was not so lucky; he had trouble finding more than a day or two of work a week. Next, he tried sharecropping—living on an established farm and growing crops for a corporate owner. This work turned out to be as grueling as migrant labor. Sharecroppers never had a day off and, in fact, they shared little in the farm's profits. After two years, the Chavezes moved off the farm.

They headed north to Crescent City near the Oregon border where Cesar and Richard found work at a lumber camp. Cesar loved the work as well as living in a cabin in the woods, but Helen soon grew weary of the pioneer life. She recalled, "We had this wood stove and you had to chop wood all the time, to cook, to keep warm, everything."

The Chavezes returned to San Jose, finding a home in a *barrio* (Spanish-speaking neighborhood in a city) known as *Sal Si Puedes*. In English, the name translates to "Get Out If You Can."

In the 1930s, while Chavez and his family journeyed from farm to farm in search of work, a much different culture was taking shape in the midwestern metropolis of Chicago. For years, the city was besieged by lawlessness led by such crime lords as Al Capone and Frank Nitti. In 1938, a young sociologist named Saul Alinsky was hired by Chicago's Institute of Juvenile Research to find out why young people chose a life of crime.

Alinksy's research soon took him to the city's Back-of-the-Yards neighborhood, an immense slum in Chicago's stockyards district. Most people who lived in the Back-of-the-Yards did not have jobs, and those people who were lucky enough to find employment were at the mercy of unscrupulous employers who would cut their wages or fire them on a whim. It did not take long for Alinsky to conclude that the endless cycle of poverty and unemployment had created a path leading to a life of crime that many young people found irresistible.

Alinsky also believed that communities had to rebuild themselves. At this point, he decided to do more than just study the deterioration of the inner cities. He changed his life's work from sociology to social activism. On July 14, 1939, Alinsky convened the first meeting of the Back-of-the-Yards Council. It was composed of neighborhood residents whose aim was to improve conditions for workers at the stockyards. The council staged a series of pickets, strikes and boycotts of the stockyards, and soon won concessions from the stockyard owners. In becoming a force in the stockyards, the council had raised the interest of organized labor unions that were eager to help. John L. Lewis, head of the Congress of Industrial Organizations, became Alinksy's mentor and provided support for the council's activities. In 1940, Alinsky decided to take his community organizing campaign national. He founded the Industrial Area Foundation (IAF).

Saul Alinsky (far left) leads a group of picketers who were part of the United Packinghouse Workers strike against Chicago's packinghouse industry in 1946. It was Saul Alinsky's and his ally Fred Ross's efforts to champion the cause of disadvantaged workers that inspired Chavez to unite farm workers.

The IAF aimed to do more than just win better wages and working conditions for laborers. The association sought to change civil rights laws, register voters, end discrimination in the workforce, root out corruption and find ways to eradicate poverty. In many cities, the IAF established local organizations to carry out its work. In San Jose, an Alinsky ally named Fred Ross started the Community Service Organization (CSO). Ross began his career in social work in the 1930s, helping displaced migrants from Oklahoma settle in California. Later, he would help resettle thousands of Japanese Americans who were interned during World War II because the government feared they could become spies or saboteurs for Japan. At the first CSO meeting in 1952, a young lumberyard worker who lived in *Sal Si Puedes* showed up to see what Ross's group was all about. That worker's name was Cesar Chavez.

"At the very first meeting I was very much impressed with

SAUL ALINSKY

The Community Service Organization was just one group that owed its existence to the spirit and vision of Saul Alinsky. Alinsky's philosophy that ordinary people could empower themselves and make changes was at the heart of the civil rights drive of the 1950s and the anti-war movement of the 1960s. His 1946 book, *Reveille for Radicals*, called on America's poor to reclaim democracy. It became a bestseller.

Alinsky organized The Woodlawn Organization that fought for civil rights on Chicago's South Side in 1959. The main weapon Alinsky employed was a massive voter registration drive that turned the poor African-American residents of the South Side into a formidable political force capable of challenging Mayor Richard J. Daley's Democratic machine.

By the 1960s, many of the campus radicals demonstrating against the war in Vietnam were employing Alinsky's methods. *Time* magazine called Alinsky "a prophet of power to the people" in 1970.

By the early 1970s, Alinsky realized that the American middle class was drifting to the right and warned poor people that they were in danger of losing the support of the nation's most important bloc of voters. He never got the chance to help the poor adapt to a more conservative society. He died suddenly of a heart attack on June 12, 1972, at the age of 63.

Cesar," Ross said. "I could tell he was intensely interested, a kind of burning interest rather than one of those inflammatory things that lasts one night and is forgotten. He asked many questions, part of it to see if I really knew, putting me to the test. But it was much more than that."

Ross asked Chavez to head a voter registration drive in San Jose. Ross was impressed with Chavez's organizational abilities as well as his personal magnetism. Chavez soon convinced many of his friends to assist in the campaign, and within a short time brought in 6,000 new registrations, most of them from *Sal Si Puedes.*

Within a few months, Chavez quit his job at the lumber-yard to become a full-time activist for the Community Service Organization. The job paid all of $35 a week, and the work was grueling—often day and night, seven days a week. But it soon started paying dividends. Ross dispatched him to Oakland, Decoto, Bakersfield, and Madera in the San Joaquin Valley where he started new CSO chapters.

It was during this period that he met the Reverend Donald McDonnell, a Catholic priest assigned to *Sal Si Puedes.* Chavez had always been a devoted Catholic; then, under McDonnell's guidance, he learned about the Catholic Church's long history of seeking social justice. Also from McDonnell, he learned the church had defended the rights of the worker. For example, in 1891, Pope Leo XIII issued his *Encyclical on Labor,* a statement in defense of the right of workers to organize into labor unions.

"Associations of workers and employers of workers are to be encouraged," wrote Leo. "These associations in whatever form they take are to encourage just wages."

Chavez also found himself interested in the story of America's labor movement. He read biographies of labor lead-ers Eugene Debs and John L. Lewis. He also read biographies of Mohandas Gandhi, who helped win independence for India from Great Britain in 1947 through the use of nonviolent civil disobedience. Later, as the civil rights movement blossomed in the South, Chavez would follow the career of the Reverend Martin Luther King, Jr. who also advocated nonviolent civil disobedience.

Chavez made another ally in Doris Huerta, who was helping to organize a CSO chapter in Los Angeles. Huerta and Chavez would soon forge a partnership that would endure for decades. She said, "The first time I really heard him speak was at a board meeting in Stockton in 1957; he had to respond to sharp questions from an attorney, and I was very impressed by the way he handled it. You couldn't tell by looking at him what he could do; you had to see him in action to appreciate him."

Indeed, Chavez hardly made an impression when he entered a room. He was short and thin, standing just five feet six inches tall and weighing little more than 175 pounds. He was usually dressed in a plaid shirt and tan pants: the uniform of the workingman, Chavez would tell people.

In 1954, the CSO decided to establish a chapter in Oxnard, a small city north of Los Angeles where many large lemon groves and vegetable farms were located. The CSO had been invited into Oxnard by the United Packinghouse Workers union, which had been unsuccessful in its efforts to organize the Mexican-American workers who were employed in the packing sheds, the places where the produce was crated and made ready for shipment. Labor leaders felt the CSO could counsel the workers on their rights and show them that they had the ability to organize and demand higher wages.

Chavez was anxious for the challenge. It would be his first chance to help organize farm workers, although it would not be as the representative of a union. Also, when Chavez was young, his family spent an uncomfortable winter in Oxnard at a lemon grove with only a tent to shelter them from the driving rains. By 1954, Cesar and Helen Chavez were parents. They found a home in Oxnard and Chavez got down to work.

Chavez quickly reached the bottom of the real problem in Oxnard: the *braceros.* They were Mexican citizens who received permission from the U.S. government to work on American

To make up for the shortage of available farm workers during the war years, the U.S. government permitted Mexican citizens, known as *braceros*, to work on farms in the United States. This photo taken in 1942 shows one such *bracero* laborer picking carrots. Farm owners continued to use the *bracero* system long after the war ended as a source of cheap labor and to deny local workers jobs.

farms. The *bracero* system started during World War II because of the labor shortage created by the military draft. When the war ended, many politically influential growers persuaded Congress to keep the *bracero* system intact, claiming that labor shortages still existed after the war. In reality, though, the growers preferred the *bracero* system because they knew they could pay Mexicans less than American farm workers would demand. In Oxnard, Chavez found many angry, unemployed farm workers complaining that growers were making use of *bracero* labor. In some cases, workers told Chavez, they were sent right home from the field when a truck full of *braceros* arrived to replace them.

"The jobs belonged to local workers," said Chavez. "*Braceros* didn't make any money, and they were exploited viciously, forced to work under conditions the local people wouldn't tolerate."

Chavez made the *bracero* system the main issue of the CSO's work in Oxnard. To obtain work, farm laborers had to first report to the local Farm Placement Service, an agency of the state government. The Farm Placement Service would then issue the workers referral cards and send them out to a farm that was hiring. Chavez learned that the referral card system was useless; workers were often issued cards, but when they showed up for work they were told they were too late and that the foreman had already hired *braceros*. He complained to U.S. Labor Department officials, pointing out that the growers were using *braceros* even though there were plenty of workers available in Oxnard. The federal government responded by investigating the claims, running surprise inspections and, in many cases, issuing citations and ordering growers to hire local workers.

He organized picket lines at *bracero* camps and demonstrations in front of the gates of farms that abused the *bracero* system. Through sources at the farms and in the government offices, Chavez learned which farms were hiring and rushed workers there in the early morning hours before the *braceros* could show up for the jobs. He also organized a voter registration drive, signing up thousands of Oxnard Mexican Americans, which made them into a political force.

After a year, the state government finally took action. The head of the Oxnard Farm Placement Service was fired and the referral card system was scrapped. The CSO also won a wage concession from the Oxnard growers, convincing them to raise the farm workers' pay from $0.65 to $0.90 an hour. Chavez told Ross that the farm workers of Oxnard were willing to join a union and offered to help organize a bargaining group, but Ross told him that the CSO had no business in unionizing laborers and that the Packinghouse Workers would take on that responsibility. Reluctantly, Chavez moved on.

"This has been a wonderful experience for me in Oxnard," Chavez told Ross. "I never dreamed that so much hell could be raised."

For the next three years, Chavez's star rose in the CSO. He helped organize 22 chapters in California. Under his guidance, thousands of Mexican Americans became registered voters. The CSO also lobbied for public improvements in *barrios*; new playgrounds were built, sidewalks were repaired, and streets were repaved. Mexican Americans started standing up for their civil rights, and soon the "Whites Only" signs came down from restaurant doors and movie theater entrances. His efforts came to the attention of Saul Alinsky, who promoted him to executive director of the national CSO.

In 1962, Chavez suddenly resigned. He felt that he had accomplished all he could do within the CSO's mission of organizing communities. His experience in Oxnard had made him realize that farm workers could never earn a decent wage unless they organized into an effective union.

The Chavezes moved to Delano where Helen had relatives. Cesar Chavez knew that a new struggle awaited them. The growers in Delano were strongly anti-union, and there was no question in Chavez's mind that his efforts to organize the farm workers there could result in violence.

Chavez later reflected on his feelings at that time toward the work that awaited him in Delano and said, "For the first time, I was frightened—I was very frightened."

Local 218

Americans first learned of the plight of the hapless migrant farm workers through the writings of author John Steinbeck, whose 1939 novel, *The Grapes of Wrath,* told of the travels of the Joad family, poor Oklahomans searching for a new beginning in California. He wrote:

> And then the dispossessed were drawn west—from Kansas, Oklahoma, Texas, New Mexico; from Nevada and Arkansas families, tribes, dusted out, tractored out. Carloads, caravans, homeless and hungry—restless as ants, scurrying to find work to do—to lift, to push, to pull, to pick, to cut—anything, any burden to bear, for food. The kids are hungry. We got no place to live. Like ants scurrying for work, for food, and most of all for land.

Many of the farm workers emigrated from Oklahoma and neighboring states, a region hit by terrible droughts in the 1930s. By 1934, the droughts were so severe that the once-fertile croplands of the

Migrant workers like this couple traveled the countryside in search of new opportunities for work. John Steinbeck's classic novel *The Grapes of Wrath*, written the same year this photo was taken in 1939, increased the public's awareness of the migrant workers' plight.

Great Plains were virtually a desert. Journalist Ernie Pyle, who would go on to become the nation's greatest war correspondent, toured northern Kansas in 1936 and wrote, "If you would like to have your heart broken, just come out here. This is dust-storm country. It is the saddest land I have ever seen."

The area was plagued by sweeping dust storms that blew walls of black soil across the plains, coating everything with a thick layer of grime. At times the storms were so bad that people had to seal up their houses and stay indoors until the winds died down. The drought was not the only cause for the storms. For decades, farmers in the plains states had misused their land, plowing under thick prairie grasses that held the topsoil in place. Grazing by cattle and sheep further depleted the grasses. An area covering about 100 million acres in Kansas, Colorado, Oklahoma, Texas, Arkansas and New Mexico was affected. In 1935, Associated Press reporter Robert Geiger dubbed the area the "Dust Bowl."

"Three little words achingly familiar on a western farmer's tongue rule life in the dust bowl of the continent—if it rains," Geiger wrote.

When the crops failed, farmers could not make their loan payments, and the banks seized their properties. Homeless, thousands of farm families then made their way to California where it was said that work was available. The Oklahomans who made the trek were derisively known as "Okies."

Sadly, the migrants were not much better off in California. Migrant labor camps were often ramshackle and unsanitary, although some camps established with government aid were a cut above the rest, such as Weedpatch Camp in Kern County. As for the work, it was backbreaking toil that paid little—when it was available.

Steinbeck illustrated the plight of the migrant workers when he wrote:

> The truck moved along the beautiful roads, past orchards where the peaches were beginning to color, past vineyards with the clusters pale and green, under lines of walnut trees whose branches spread half across the road. At each entrance-gate Al slowed; and at each gate there was a sign: "No help wanted. No trespassing."
>
> Al said, "'Pa, they's boun' to be work when them fruits gets ready. Funny place—they tell ya they ain't no work 'fore you ask 'em." He drove slowly on.

While the Okies, the Arkies from Arkansas and migrant farm workers from other states searched dejectedly for work in

California's fruit belt, trouble was brewing in Los Angeles. For years, Mexican immigrants had been settling in the Los Angeles *barrio*. Race relations were touchy. By the 1940s, there were often clashes between whites and Mexicans, who were called "zoot suiters" by the whites because of the flashy clothes they wore that were in vogue at the time. Violence erupted on June 7, 1943, when several thousand whites, including many soldiers and sailors on leave, rioted in Los Angeles, assaulted Mexican Americans and vandalized their homes and businesses. The incident became known as the "zoot suit riots."

Wrote eyewitness Al Waxman, editor of the *Eastside Journal*: "At Twelfth and Central I came upon a scene that will long live in my memory . . . four boys came out of a pool hall. They were wearing the zoot suits that have become the symbol of the fighting flag. Police ordered them into arrest cars. One

JOHN STEINBECK

John Steinbeck is arguably America's most important literary voice of the twentieth century. Winner of both the Nobel and Pulitzer prizes, Steinbeck's literature opened a nation's eyes to the hard edges of rural life.

He was born in 1902 in Salinas, California, a region where he centered many of his stories. As a youth, he worked as a farm laborer and ranch hand, experiences he called on when he later wrote *The Grapes of Wrath* as well as other stories of farm life, including *Of Mice and Men*, *Tortilla Flat* and *The Red Pony*.

He wrote more than just stories of farm life. During World War II, he authored *The Moon is Down*, about the Nazi occupation of Norway, and the script for *Lifeboat*, a film directed by Alfred Hitchcock. Other books included *East of Eden*, *The Winter of Our Discontent* and *The Pearl*.

His final book, a modernization of the King Arthur legend entitled *The Acts of King Arthur and His Noble Knights*, was published in 1975, seven years after his death.

Paul Acevedo (center) stands among fellow "zoot suiters" after escaping the rioting mob that beat him. Acevedo is one of many Mexican Americans targeted in the "zoot suit riots" of 1943, so named for the flashy dress suits worn by young Mexican Los Angelinos.

refused. He asked: 'Why am I being arrested?' The police officer answered with three swift blows of the nightstick across the boy's head and he went down. As he sprawled, he was kicked in the face. . . . At the next corner a Mexican mother cried out, 'Don't take my boy, he did nothing. He's only 15 years old. Don't take him.' She was struck across the jaw with a night-stick and almost dropped the 2 1/2-year-old baby that was clinging in her arms."

California is a state blessed with a temperate climate and abundant sunshine, enabling growers the luxury of a year-round planting season. It is not unusual for a single farm field to produce two or three harvests a year. With that much potential in the soil, many workers are needed for the fields.

California growers started relying on immigrant labor in the 1870s. At the time, there was a great influx of Chinese immigrants into the state. Because of racism, the Chinese found themselves unwelcome in the cities. So the Chinese became a ready and willing labor pool for farm work. Sadly, the racism followed the Chinese to the farms. In the 1880s, Congress passed laws severely limiting access to jobs by Chinese immigrants. That reduced the number of farm jobs open to the Chinese. In the 1890s, the jobs became even scarcer when an economic recession made farm work attractive to white laborers.

By the early twentieth century, a new immigrant labor pool was available to the growers: the Japanese. Japanese immigrants were willing to work for incredibly low wages—sometimes only $0.35 or $0.40 a day. Within a few years the Japanese became unwelcome visitors, too. It seemed that the Japanese planned on owning their own farms. Once Japanese immigrants started buying up land in California, government and industry officials responded with alarm.

"The Chinese when they were here were ideal," reported the California Fruit Growers' Convention of 1907. "They were patient, plodding and uncomplaining in the performance of a most menial service. They submitted to everything, never violating a contract. The Japanese now coming in are a tricky and cunning lot, who break contracts and become quite independent. They are not organized into unions, but their clannishness seems to operate as a union would. One trick is to contract work at a certain price and then in the rush of the harvest season to strike unless wages are raised."

Congress addressed the Japanese in 1924, passing laws that

prohibited Japanese immigration. Of course, relations between the United States and Japan continued to deteriorate over the next two decades leading up to World War II.

Mexicans, Filipinos, Puerto Ricans and Hindus from India arrived in the 1920s. African Americans migrating from the South also supplied workers to the fields. White vagabonds needing a place to bunk down for a few days were willing to do the work as well. Many growers paid different wage scales for different races. Regardless of whether a Filipino or Mexican worked in the fields, though, wages were kept as low as possible.

During the 1930s, the labor pool deepened with the arrival of the Okies, Arkies and others from the Dust Bowl. With the start of World War II, what had been a farm labor surplus was suddenly a shortage as most young American men were drafted into the service or were able to find jobs in the war industries. And so started the *bracero* program—the importation of cheap labor from Mexico to work in the farm fields. *Braceros* signed contracts in Mexico to work in the United States and were given permission to remain in America until their contracts expired—usually at the end of the harvest. That is how the system was supposed to work, but many of the large growers found another source of cheap labor: illegal Mexican immigrants who had slipped across the border and were willing to work for little more than slave wages. Known derisively as "line jumpers" or "wetbacks," because many of them waded across the Rio Grande River on the Texas-Mexico border, these workers were often abused.

Frequently, growers would give them jobs, food and places to live until the crop was harvested; then, the growers would alert federal immigration authorities and have the hapless Mexicans deported so they would not have to pay them. By 1948, it was believed that roughly 60,000 illegal aliens from Mexico were living in California, many of them working on farms. The illegal aliens lucky enough to be paid could expect wages of no more than a few cents an hour. Their labor was much cheaper than that of the *braceros* who could earn $0.30 an hour.

Steelworkers on strike line up to receive bread in 1937. These workers were among the 8.5 million Americans who had organized into unions by 1940, using collective bargaining to improve work conditions.

By the early 1900s, trade unionism had become a part of the fabric of American life. As the country moved toward industrialization, workers found it was to their benefit to form organizations and bargain collectively for better wages and working conditions. Industrial leaders did not give in easily. Often, unionization was not accomplished until after long strikes that frequently resulted in violence and bloodshed. Nevertheless, by World War II, mineworkers, steelworkers, autoworkers, railroad workers and members of dozens of other trades were unionized. By 1940, about 8.5 million American workers belonged to unions.

However, most farm workers were not unionized. Efforts to start farm workers' unions, particularly in California, had failed.

Growers refused to deal with union representatives, running them off the land if they tried to organize workers. Most of the workers were migrants who were in the area only for a few weeks or months until the harvest was in. Therefore, it was difficult to form the regional union chapters known as "locals" that would do the actual bargaining for the members.

As a boy, Cesar Chavez recalled living in northern California when he first learned of the existence of the agricultural unions. He said, "We were living in San Jose. One of the old [Congress of Industrial Organizations] unions began organizing workers in the dried-fruit industry, so my father and uncle became members. Sometimes the men would meet at our house and I remember seeing their picket signs and hearing them talk. They had a strike and my father and uncle picketed at night. It made a deep impression on me. But of course they lost the strike, and that was the end of the union. But from that time on, my father joined every new agricultural union that came along."

After World War II, efforts to unionize farm workers were renewed. In 1947, organizers for the National Farm Labor Union (NFLU) visited Kern County, California, and concluded that working conditions at the huge DiGiorgio Fruit Corporation were prime for unionization.

DiGiorgio was the largest crop producer in Kern County, growing some $18 million worth of fruits and vegetables in 1946 at its two farms, located near Arvin and Delano. The company owned farms in other states as well as produce auction houses. In addition to fruit and vegetable crops, DiGiorgio raised cotton and cattle and owned several oil wells. Joseph DiGiorgio, a wealthy and influential grower, headed the company.

On his farms, workers toiled for wages as low as $0.80 an hour. Shifts could last as long as 15 hours, but DiGiorgio paid no bonuses for overtime. There were usually no breaks during the day—workers ate as they picked. Work weeks could extend for seven days if necessary. Many of the workers had to use the notorious short hoe, a stubby digging tool that forced its user to work in a bent-over position. After 15 hours bent over a short hoe, workers returned to their homes aching and exhausted. Later, many states outlawed the short hoe.

Housing was poor as well. By then, many of the farm workers had been in California for a decade or more and had put down roots. But few owned their own homes; instead, they were forced to rent cottages from the growers. Others working at DiGiorgio lived in ramshackle camps, bunkhouses and even old railroad cars. Filipino immigrants had by then joined the labor pool of Mexican Americans and former Dust Bowl inhabitants on the DiGiorgio farms.

Considering conditions such as those in existence at DiGiorgio, it is little wonder that the NFLU was able to obtain more than 1,200 signatures on union authorization cards from farm workers in Kern County. With about 900 of its new members employed at DiGiorgio, the new union was dubbed Arvin Local 218 of the National Farm Labor Union. NFLU national headquarters dispatched Hank Hasiwar, a veteran organizer, to Kern County to help the union negotiate its first contract.

On September 22, 1947, Hasiwar notified owner Joseph DiGiorgio that a majority of his 1,300 workers had designated Local 218 as their collective bargaining agent and that he was ready to commence negotiations on a contract. Hasiwar said the union planned to demand a $0.10 an hour wage hike, a grievance procedure, and pay raises and promotions based on seniority. DiGiorgio, who wanted no union on his property, refused to even meet with Hasiwar.

On September 30, Hasiwar convened a meeting of Local 218 and took a strike authorization vote. The membership approved the strike by an overwhelming majority, voting to walk off their jobs the next day.

In the early morning hours of October 1, picketers arrived at the gates of the DiGiorgio farms. The walkout left DiGiorgio with just 200 workers in a business that ordinarily employed some 1,300 people. DiGiorgio decided to dig in, though, and the standoff commenced.

Most of the workers who stayed on their jobs at DiGiorgio

were *braceros*. The *braceros* sympathized with the union members, but they knew that if they walked off their jobs they would be deported. The union complained, but federal officials refused to remove the *braceros* from the DiGiorgio farm, arguing that a labor strike could not be used as cause to deport an immigrant worker.

Therefore, in the first critical weeks of the strike, DiGiorgio was able to keep its produce moving with just a fraction of its workforce. While the union pressed the case against the *braceros*, DiGiorgio recruited other workers from Kern County. The company also found hundreds of illegal immigrants willing to work. By early January, the workforce at DiGiorgio was back up to about 800 laborers.

The union also made a grave tactical error by scheduling the strike to begin in October. By then, most of the produce was already out of the fields. The activity was moving to the farms' packinghouses, which required less manpower. There is no question that Local 218 was able to severely damage DiGiorgio's business in 1947 and 1948, but the company found a way to operate, and DiGiorgio never found itself in such economic distress that it had to give in and bargain.

Nevertheless, for months it appeared the union would prevail. Local 218 had few financial resources to help its members survive a long strike, but the cause soon came to the attention of labor leaders elsewhere and help flowed in. The Central Labor Council of Bakersfield, California, endorsed the strike and told its members not to buy DiGiorgio products. Teamsters from Los Angeles and San Francisco refused to drive trucks onto the farms, which meant DiGiorgio had to scramble to find independent truckers willing to haul its produce. The Retail Clerks Union of Los Angeles also honored the strike; its members refused to stock store shelves with DiGiorgio products. The Kern County Central Labor Committee established a strike fund, and in a little more than a year collected nearly $90,000, most of it donated by union members outside of California.

In May 1948, Bertha Rankin, a Kern County ranch owner and union sympathizer, donated an acre of her property to Local 218 so the union could establish a permanent headquarters. In a short time, Local 218 had its own union hall; since its founding the previous fall, the union had been operating out of a trailer parked in the backyard of a member.

Union leaders in San Francisco organized caravans that delivered food, cash and clothing to striking DiGiorgio workers. In early 1948, NFLU President H. L. Mitchell defiantly announced: "We propose to keep a picket line about the DiGiorgio ranch indefinitely and turn our attention to other areas of the state to break through the solid front of the agricultural employers."

And still, DiGiorgio refused to bargain. The company officially notified the leaders of Local 218 that they had been fired. Violence occasionally broke out on the picket lines. Kern County deputy sheriffs, who had been assigned to maintain law and order at the company gates, were known to look the other way when thugs were dispatched by the company to rough up the strikers.

On February 8, 1948, five strikers walking the picket line were assaulted by attackers who rushed them from the farm property. When word of the assault spread among the union ranks, dozens of members showed up at the farm gates armed and ready to fight back. Hasiwar managed to calm them and send everyone home.

But there was vandalism committed against the company's property. Union members cut down fruit trees and trucks were pelted with rocks. Over the course of the strike, several union members were jailed on vandalism charges.

Next, DiGiorgio tried to stir up anti-communist sentiment against the strikers. At the time, the world was living at the dawn of the Cold War; Americans feared communists and soon the federal government, under the direction of powerful Senator Joseph McCarthy, would violate the rights of many innocent Americans, accusing them of communist sympathies. In Kern County, the company asked the California Legislature to investigate the NFLU for communist influences. "All this agitation is

H. L. Mitchell, president of the National Farm Labor Union, testified before the Senate Labor Committee in 1949 that his union had been wronged when the Taft-Hartley Act, which involves the government in labor disputes, was used to break his union's strike against the DiGiorgio Fruit Company.

communist inspired by subversive elements," declared Joseph DiGiorgio. A state senate committee held hearings and eventually concluded that communists had not infiltrated the NFLU. Still, the senate probe gave the union one more battle to keep it occupied while DiGiorgio searched for a way to deliver its produce to the markets.

The strike continued and so did the violence. In May 1948, with the strike in its eighth month, Local 218 President James Price was wounded in the neck when drive-by shooters sprayed a union hall meeting with gunfire. No arrests were ever made.

On October 1, 1948, the strike celebrated its first anniversary. The company managed to get its harvest out of the fields without the striking workers. In Hollywood, filmmakers employed by the NFLU produced a documentary about the strike entitled *Poverty in the Land of Plenty*. DiGiorgio claimed union leaders lied about the company in the film and filed a lawsuit alleging libel against H. L. Mitchell. The lawsuit demanded damages in excess of $2 million. By then, Mitchell's union was virtually bankrupt; the organization had no money to defend against the lawsuit or pay the damages should it lose in court. DiGiorgio offered to drop the lawsuit if Mitchell called off the strike.

On May 9, 1949, Mitchell sent a telegram to Hasiwar announcing that the strike was over. There would be no union contract for the DiGiorgio farm workers.

The farm workers of Kern County may have lost the battle, but the war was far from over. The 20-month DiGiorgio strike proved that the farm workers would stick together through the worst of times. And, they had dropped the old ethnic barriers that had kept them apart in years gone by. Mexican Americans, African Americans, Filipinos and whites had walked together on the picket lines in Kern County.

Even H. L. Mitchell refused to concede defeat. When he recalled the picketers, Mitchell said, "We are just ending the first round."

When the Eagle Flies

The first meeting of the National Farm Workers Association was called to order on Sunday, September 30, 1962, in a movie theater in Fresno, California. Cesar Chavez convened the meeting because his efforts to organize the farm workers had been going so well that he felt it was time to solidify the membership by calling them together for a convention. Indeed, in just six months, Chavez had distributed 80,000 invitations to migrant farm workers, and the vast majority of them returned the cards, indicating a willingness to join the union.

There was a lot of business to conduct at the meeting. First on the agenda was the election of officers. Chavez was named president of the union. Dolores Huerta, who left the Community Service Organization to help organize the union, was named a vice president. Two other organizers, Gil Padilla and Julio Hernandez, were also named vice presidents. Cesar's cousin, Manuel Chavez, was elected secretary-treasurer. Dues were set at $3.50 a month,

Chavez called together the first meeting of the United Farm Workers in 1962. This first meeting established membership, dues and an emblem, the "Aztec eagle," that simultaneously represented the union's strength and its mostly Mexican-American membership.

and it was decided that the dues would go mostly into a life insurance fund for union members.

At this point, Chavez decided it was much too early to confront the growers. Although thousands of farm workers had signed union authorization cards, getting them to actually join the organization and pay dues would be another matter. Farm workers were still mostly migrants, and the formation of union locals would prove to be a major challenge for the NFWA. At the Fresno convention, for example, just 212 farm workers had shown up.

Chavez was well aware of the sad history of organizing farm workers, particularly in the 1940s when the National Farm Labor Union failed to win a contract with DiGiorgio. Chavez believed it would take years for the new organization to develop the resources and muscle necessary to endure a long strike. Instead, Chavez said the NFWA would be far better off lobbying legislators in the California Assembly for a law setting a minimum wage for farm workers. At the time, farm workers were earning no more than $0.90 an hour. Chavez thought the union would be justified in asking the legislators for a minimum wage of $1.50 an hour.

There was one final piece of business to be decided at the first convention. Manuel Chavez and Cesar's brother, Richard, had taken on the job of designing a symbol for the NFWA. Working with a Latin-American, Los Angeles-based artist, they designed an emblem that featured a square-edged thunderbird with its wings spread wide, standing over the initials "NFWA." The union membership's Mexican heritage would be represented in the design: upside down, the thunderbird resembled an Aztec pyramid. Eventually, union members would refer to the symbol as the "Aztec eagle."

They showed the emblem to Cesar who suggested one modification.

"What Cesar didn't like was that I had two little feet on the thunderbird—they looked like chicken feet," recalled Richard Chavez. "It just didn't look good."

A straight bar replaced the little bird feet. Cesar chose the colors: white for hope, black for the struggle of the farm workers and red for the sacrifices that awaited them.

The emblem was shown to the farm workers at the Fresno convention, and they voted overwhelmingly to adopt it as the symbol of the new National Farm Workers of America.

"When that damn eagle flies, we'll have a union," declared Manuel Chavez.

Cesar, Helen and their children had arrived in Delano six months before. They withdrew their life savings of $1,200 from the bank and quickly spent it all as Cesar traveled up and down the coast in his recruiting efforts. To help make ends meet, Helen Chavez returned to the Delano fields where she picked grapes. Still, the family struggled. Often, when Cesar Chavez visited a farm worker family to sign them up as members of the union, he would ask them to make a donation of food so that he could feed his own family that night. Surprisingly, Chavez found the farm workers were more than willing to help. Suspicious of union organizers who had visited them in the past but failed to make good on their promises, they opened their hearts to a man humble enough to beg for food. To the farm workers, it showed that this man was not interested in personal gain.

"We didn't have any money at all, none for gas and hardly any for food. So I started asking for food. It turned out to be the best thing I could have done, although at first it's hard on your pride. Some of our best members came in that way. If people give you their food, they'll give you their hearts," Chavez said.

As Chavez drove from farm to farm, he learned that he had competition from the Agricultural Workers Organizing Committee (AWOC), a bargaining unit that was formed by the huge American Federation of Labor-Congress of Industrial Organizations (AFL-CIO). Over the years, the AFL-CIO repeatedly tried to organize California farm workers and always failed. It had led dozens of walkouts at California farms, but the growers were always able to carry on without the union members. The growers broke the strikes much the same way that DiGiorgio was able to survive in the 1940s: by hiring nonunion strikebreakers known as scabs, making use of *braceros* and employing illegal immigrants. Rarely had the AFL-CIO's efforts ever resulted in more than just a token increase in wages.

One of the AFL-CIO's biggest mistakes had been its failure to make use of Mexican-American organizers. Although farm workers were white, black and Asian, Mexican Americans were by far the largest ethnic group working in the fields. Chavez found that Mexican Americans were suspicious of the white AFL-CIO organizers and much preferred signing on with his union.

It seemed that wherever Chavez traveled, he found farm workers willing to join the union. "I left Stockton at 2:30 A.M. and arrived in Delano at 6:30 A.M.," he wrote during his travels that first year. "Saw a crew on the road in Tipton and stopped long enough to register them—to drop off more cards."

But while Chavez found many potential union members, he also heard many horror stories about the lives of farm workers. In 1960, the state government in California reported that roughly 25 percent of farm workers did not own a refrigerator and, therefore, had no place in their homes to keep food fresh. Twenty-five percent of farm worker families did not have flush toilets in their homes. Half of the farm worker families did not have a fresh water tap in their homes. More than half of their children had not been inoculated against polio.

By 1965, although the California farming industry was registering a gross income of some $4 billion, the farm workers were living in poverty. The average annual wage for a farm worker that year was $1,350 or well below the federal poverty level of $3,100. Overtime pay, paid holidays, vacations, sick leave, pensions and unemployment insurance payments—all standard benefits available to most American workers—were unheard of in the world of migrant farm labor.

In 1964, the farm labor movement scored a major victory when the U.S. Congress let the law authorizing the *bracero* program expire. Throughout the 1950s, the growers had successfully lobbied Congress to keep the program intact, arguing that a labor shortage existed in the farm fields. Union leaders objected, but their complaints went unheeded in Washington.

By the early 1960s, the mood in Washington had changed. Power in Congress had by then shifted to the cities, which

These farmers perform "stoop labor," bending over with a short hoe for as much as 15 hours. Remaining in this hunched position for long periods of time caused many migrant workers lifelong back pain. This type of unusually backbreaking work is but one example of the type of extremely harsh work that farm laborers were expected to perform, and for which Chavez believed they should be adequately compensated.

usually sent liberal-minded representatives and senators to Washington. Many of these lawmakers owed their elections to politically active union organizers. When the unions complained about the *braceros*, there were new people in Congress willing to listen. In 1964, there were 65,000 *braceros* working on farm fields in California. In 1965, just 1,000 *braceros* remained in the country, fulfilling the final months of their contracts.

The disappearance of the *braceros* emboldened the farm workers' unions. In 1965, Chavez's union had 1,700 dues-paying members, giving it enough muscle to stage a small strike and win pay raises for workers at two Delano rose farms.

"A farm worker from McFarland came to see me," Chavez recalled. "He said he was sick and tired of how people working the roses were being treated, and he was 'willing to go the limit.' The people wanted union representation, but the real issue, as in most cases when you begin, was wages. They were promised $9 for a thousand, but they were actually getting $6.50 and $7 for grafting roses. Most of them signed cards and gave us the right to bargain for them."

The strike lasted four days. The company quickly caved in and agreed to a wage increase. Months later, a second grower agreed to new terms. Despite those modest victories, Chavez still believed his union was too small to take on any of the major growers and he discouraged talk of a wide-scale job action in his ranks.

But the competing union, the AWOC, believed it had the resources to call a strike. Then led by Larry Itliong, a Filipino immigrant, the AWOC had been unable to convince many Mexican Americans to join its ranks. Instead, Itliong concentrated on recruiting fellow immigrants from the Philippines.

The AWOC called a strike on September 8, 1965, at vineyards in Kern and Tulare counties when growers refused to consider a wage increase. At the time, Filipino workers could count on wages of no more than $1 an hour, and few of them were guaranteed work for more than a few months a year.

Unlike the NFWA, Itliong's group had the resources of the powerful AFL-CIO behind it. That meant there would be a strike fund for the workers and support from other unions. Still, Itliong knew the strike was doomed to failure unless the Mexican Americans agreed not to cross the picket lines. Even without the *braceros*, there was no shortage of labor in the Delano area.

Itliong approached Chavez and asked the NFWA to recognize the strike. For Cesar Chavez and the NFWA, Itliong's plea represented a turning point. The two unions had never been close allies. Itliong had twice offered Chavez's workers the opportunity to come under the AWOC umbrella. Both times, Chavez was able to convince his workers to resist the idea of a merger. Chavez was hesitant to commit his organization to a strike that he didn't control. He said, "That morning of September 8, a strike was the furthest thing from my mind. The first I heard of it was when people came to me and said the Filipinos had gone out . . . all I could think was, 'Oh God, we're not ready for a strike.'"

On the other hand, Chavez felt a responsibility to let the union members vote on Itliong's request. Many leaders of the NFWA felt their union should support the Filipinos. After all, they argued, regardless of the differences between the two unions, they had a common mission: better wages for farm workers. Chavez was surprised to find that one of the pro-strike NFWA members was his wife, Helen. "Well, what are we? Aren't we a union?" she asked her husband. "That's what we're a union for, right?"

On September 16, Cesar Chavez stood in front of a meeting of NFWA members in Delano and called for a strike vote. During his speech to the Mexican-American members, Chavez told them about the beginnings of the Mexican Revolution in 1810 when a Catholic priest named Miguel Hidalgo led an uprising against the Spaniards.

"A hundred and fifty-five years ago, in the state of Guanajoto in Mexico, a padre proclaimed the struggle for liberty," Chavez said. "He was killed, but 10 years later Mexico won its independence. We Mexicans here in the United States, as well as all other farm workers, are engaged in another struggle for the freedom and dignity which poverty denies us. But it must not be a violent struggle, even if violence is used against us. Violence can only hurt us and our cause. The law is for us as well as the ranchers. The Filipinos began the strike, but it is not exclusively for them. Tonight we must decide if we are to join our fellow workers."

The vote was unanimous. On Monday morning, September 20, the NFWA joined the Filipinos on the picket line. Because there were far more Mexican Americans than Filipinos involved in the walkout, leadership of the strike passed from Itliong to Chavez.

At first, the grape growers dug in and refused to talk to the farm workers. Just days after the strike started, the growers offered a minor concession, raising the base pay for a picker just $0.20 an hour. Chavez told his people to stay on the picket lines. In the early days of the strike, it was believed that about 2,000 workers stayed off their jobs.

The strike often turned violent. At one farm, a foreman angrily confronted picketers, grabbed one of their signs and blasted it with a shotgun. At another farm, picketers were show-ered with pesticides and threatened with dogs. Other strikers were assaulted. Police seemed more interested in harassing the strikers than in guaranteeing their safety.

"Those early days were really mean," said Chavez. "We had cops stationed at our office and at our homes around the clock. Every time I got in the car in Delano, they'd follow me around, and I wouldn't shake them until I was well past several towns."

On October 19, 1965, Helen Chavez and 43 other picketers were arrested at a farm near Delano when they refused a sheriff's orders to stop shouting, "Huelga! Huelga!" It appeared that even the strikers' freedom of speech was being curtailed.

Chavez seized the opportunity. He had known from the beginning that the only way to make the strike work was to widen its scope out of Kern and Tulare counties. On the same day his wife and the others were arrested, he gave a speech at the Berkeley campus of the University of California, where the students had just been through a long and ultimately victori-ous campaign to win the right of free speech on campus. When Chavez told them that 44 picketers had been arrested for exercising their right to free speech, the students rose in unison and started shouting "Huelga! Huelga! Huelga!"

Next, the students sent dozens of telegrams to the Delano police, protesting the arrests. Chavez soon went on a lecture tour of area colleges and found himself awash in cash donations and volunteers. On one occasion, more than 350 people gathered

Walter Reuther (center), president of the United Auto Workers, walks with Cesar Chavez (left) and a group of striking grape pickers in December 1965. The recognition from the UAW, a large and powerful organization, made it difficult for the grape growers to ignore the farm workers.

outside the Kern County Courthouse to protest the charges that had been filed against the Delano 44. Eventually, the sheriff had no choice but to drop the charges.

During the turbulent 1960s, student protests were always news. Reporters soon discovered the story behind the Delano arrests, and then the strike against the growers found its way onto the front pages of newspapers. Important union leaders also took notice. Walter Reuther, the influential president of the United Auto Workers (UAW), paid a visit to Delano to support the strike.

"This is not your strike, this is our strike!" Reuther declared to a packed union hall in Delano.

Reuther pledged more than just spiritual support. He announced that the UAW would provide $7,500 a month to the farm workers' strike fund for the duration of the walkout.

The strike also drew national press when Chavez led a 300-mile march from Delano to the state capital of Sacramento to dramatize the plight of the farm workers. Chavez labeled the march the *Perigrinacion* or "Pilgrimage." The marchers would stop in migrant camps and *barrios* along the way where they would pray and share fellowship with farm workers. The ragtag marchers participating in the *Perigrinacion* started their

WALTER REUTHER

Walter Reuther's support for the farm workers helped them maintain the strike during some of their most difficult times. At the time he visited Delano and offered his help to Cesar Chavez, Reuther was perhaps America's most influential labor leader.

Born in 1907 in Wheeling, West Virginia, Reuther worked first as a steelworker, and then moved to Detroit where he found employment in the auto industry. Soon after arriving in Detroit, he started agitating for a union and was fired by the Ford Motor Company for his union work.

By the mid-1930s, he was leading strikes as president of a United Auto Workers local in Detroit. In 1936, he was instrumental in convincing General Motors to recognize the UAW. Five years later, Ford caved in and agreed to negotiate. Reuther was elected president of the national union in 1946 and remained in that post until his death in a plane crash in 1970.

Reuther is recognized as an innovative contract negotiator. Rather than concentrate only on wage demands, Reuther helped negotiate some of the first contracts for workers that included pension and profit sharing plans. He used his union's influence to lobby for civil rights, affordable housing, health care and pollution control.

journey on March 17, 1966. Dozens of marchers participated; some dropped out after a few hours, but others took their places. A few marchers, including Chavez and Larry Itliong, made the entire journey. Everywhere the marchers went, they shouted *"Huelga!"* to the bystanders who gathered along the roads to watch, and very often the word *"Huelga!"* was shouted back. The march was scheduled to end on April 10—Easter Sunday—when the marchers presented their grievances to Governor Edmund "Pat" Brown.

Just a few days' march outside of Sacramento, Chavez received word that Schenley Industries, owner of one of the farms that had been struck, was ready to give in and negotiate a contract. Schenley was a winery and distiller and had been hit hard by the strike. Outside of Kern County, Teamsters refused to carry Schenley products in their trucks. Rumors were also circulating that bartenders' unions would refuse to handle Schenley liquors and wines.

Chavez left the march and hurried to Los Angeles where an attorney for Schenley was willing to draw up a contract. After a few hours of heated negotiations—talks in which Chavez nearly walked out—a labor agreement was reached. Schenley agreed to recognize the NFWA as the union representing its workers. The company also agreed to a raise of $0.35 an hour for the workers.

After negotiating the contract, Chavez rushed back to rejoin the *Perigrinacion*. The march ended on time in Sacramento on Easter weekend, although Governor Brown was a no-show. Fresh from his triumph at the bargaining table with Schenley, Chavez proclaimed that a new day had commenced for California farm workers.

"You cannot close your eyes and your ears to us any longer," he declared that day in Sacramento. "You cannot pretend we do not exist. You cannot plead ignorance to our problems because we are here and we embody our needs for you. And we are not alone."

However, the contract with Schenley and the triumphant

Chavez leads the 300-mile march from Delano to California's capital, Sacramento, that he called the *Perigrinacion* (Pilgrimage) in the spring of 1966. The union workers marched to emphasize the importance of the grievances they presented to California's then-governor, Edmund "Pat" Brown, when they reached the capital.

arrival in Sacramento would register as just two minor victories in what was shaping up to be a long and ugly war. Soon, DiGiorgio would resort to the ploy of enlisting the Teamsters to break the strike, and although that effort would eventually fail, it would strain the NFWA's limited resources and draw the strike out further. Following Schenley's lead, other wineries in Kern and Tulare counties agreed to contracts. But the table grape growers, which harvested far more crops than the wineries, remained steadfast in their refusal to negotiate. The table grape growers were also managing to harvest their crops by making use of scab labor and illegal immigrants. By the end of 1967, there appeared to be no resolution in sight.

That is when the farm workers rested their hopes on a single word: boycott.

To Suffer
for Others

Cesar Chavez had called product boycotts before, but for the most part the boycotts had been observed only by other union members sympathetic to the farm workers' cause. For example, Teamsters had previously refused to drive trucks carrying produce grown on California farms, and members of the Retail Clerks Union refused to stock store shelves with those products. While the boycotts certainly had an impact on sales, many of the growers had been able to weather the storms. Usually, they were able to wait out the boycotts or find nonunion labor willing to drive trucks and meet their other needs. Often, the boycotts were brief and generally unknown outside the labor community.

At that point, Chavez envisioned a national boycott on table grapes. Not only would he ask other unions to observe the boycott, but he would also call on consumers to join the cause.

By then, the National Farm Workers Association had merged with the Agricultural Workers Organizing Committee. Chavez was elected

Leading a protest at a Seattle Safeway grocery store in 1969, Chavez (front right, holding sign) hoped to expand awareness of the poor conditions of California's farm workers into the public realm. He urged people to buy only produce that carried the "Aztec eagle," which indicated that it had been picked by union workers.

president of the new union that was to be called the United Farm Workers Organizing Committee. Larry Itliong was named vice president of the new organization.

The contracts Chavez's union signed with the wineries

represented a victory for the workers, but there was still much to be done. The wineries employed just 5,000 of California's 384,000 farm workers.

The table grape growers refused to sign. Table grapes were among the most important crops grown in California, representing approximately 30 percent of the state's agricultural production at the time. Ninety percent of all table grapes consumed in the United States are grown in California, and most of those grapes are grown within a 400-square-mile area around Delano. In 1968, the grape region around Delano produced some 180,000 tons of grapes a year.

Chavez had actually expected the table grape growers to cave in before the wineries. Unlike grapes that are grown to be crushed and fermented into wine, the appearance of table grapes affects their value. Certainly, shoppers in supermarkets or at produce stands do not want to pick out a bunch of grapes that are over-ripe or containing bruises. It means the bunches have to be picked carefully and on time. Chavez believed the table grape growers would be less likely to endure a long strike and more willing to come to terms with the union. As it turned out, that was not the case.

In 1968, the largest table grape grower in California was Giumarra Vineyards, which farmed roughly 5,000 acres near Delano. Giumarra had been among the most hostile of the growers against unionization of the farm workers. The company employed about 5,000 farm workers, but during the strike brought in scabs, including workers hired in Mexico. In late 1967, Chavez called for a boycott of Giumarra grapes, but the company found ways to beat the boycott. Giumarra struck deals with other growers, enabling it to ship its grapes under other labels. Chavez concluded that to truly make the boycott against Giumarra work, all table grapes had to be boycotted.

Chavez organized the boycott by drafting 200 farm workers off the picket lines and sending them to more than 30 cities in America and Canada to publicize the boycott. The union

Chavez spoke to local labor unions across the country in his efforts to orchestrate a large-scale boycott against the grape industry. By gathering nationwide support for the underpaid pickers, Chavez strengthened the boycott's effectiveness.

paid these workers little—at times, just a few dollars a week. They used their own savings, hitchhiked instead of taking planes or buses, and relied on friends and supporters to provide meals and a place to stay. In most of the cities, sympathetic unions permitted the farm workers to use their offices and telephones.

The 1960s was a volatile era in American life. In the cities, African Americans demanded their civil rights. On college campuses, students voiced their concerns about social ills and united in opposition to the Vietnam War. Nearly everywhere in America, people were beginning to question authority. That was the atmosphere in which the farm workers started speaking up for their rights, and their cause was quickly embraced by the American people.

The farm workers fanned out in the cities where they handed out leaflets in supermarket parking lots, spoke to church groups, or sought out supporters on college campuses. In Boston, farm workers staged a "Boston Grape Party." The farm workers organized a march through city streets, ending at Boston Harbor, where several bushels of Delano grapes were dumped into the water. In New York, the Transport Workers Union, which represents subway employees, printed and distributed a million leaflets announcing the boycott and found volunteers to distribute them on the city subway platforms. Eventually, 50 million leaflets admonishing people to "Boycott Grapes" were distributed in North America.

In Los Angeles, entertainer Steven Allen lent his name to the boycott. Other celebrities joined as well. Folk singers Peter, Paul and Mary and women's rights advocate Gloria Steinem announced their support for the boycott, as did civil rights leader Reverend Ralph Abernathy. Among the political leaders who signed on were U.S. senators Robert Kennedy and Jacob Javits of New York and George McGovern of South Dakota. Later in the year, Kennedy would announce his candidacy for the presidency.

Elsewhere, many politicians lined up on the side of the growers. The new governor of California, Ronald Reagan, called the boycott "immoral" and "attempted blackmail." U.S. Senator George Murphy of California said the boycott was "dishonest." Under the administration of President Richard

M. Nixon, the Defense Department stepped up its purchase of grapes to feed servicemen fighting in Vietnam as well as soldiers serving on bases in the United States.

The government may have been shipping grapes to Vietnam, but very often the fruit failed to find its way to the mess tents. During the war, there were reports that navy crewmembers sympathetic to the farm workers tossed the grapes overboard on their way to Southeast Asia.

Elsewhere, people embraced the boycott. In New Hampshire, students at the prestigious St. Paul's prep school refused to touch the grapes that were put on the dining hall tables. In New York City, Boston, Detroit and St. Louis, the mayors directed their city purchasing departments not to buy California grapes. In New York, union leader Dolores Huerta led a busload of 50 farm workers on a wintertime picket line.

"The first day we went out on the picket line, one of the Filipino women fell down and hit her head on some ice and had amnesia for about an hour," Huerta recalled. "Everybody was slipping on the ice and falling. But they had a heck of a lot of spirit."

From Delano, farm workers would follow trains carrying grapes from town to town and alert local union leaders when a shipment arrived in their city. The labor leaders would then throw up a picket line at the rail yard.

Chavez was, of course, totally immersed in *La Causa*—the cause. Cesar, Helen and their eight children continued to live in their modest Delano home. The only salary Chavez drew from the union was $10 a week. Food for the Chavez family was donated or grown in a small garden next to the Delano house. The Chavez children learned to go without new clothes and new shoes. They rarely saw their father. His union work kept him on the job 16 hours a day.

Chavez refused to draw a higher salary even though other unions were supporting the cause of the United Farm Workers financially. During the Delano strike, the United Auto Workers contributed $7,500 a month to Chavez's union while the

AFL-CIO provided $10,000 a month to the organization.

By early 1968, Chavez was clearly weary of the pace as well as the poverty, but not ready to give in.

"Either the union will be destroyed or they will sign a contract," Chavez told a reporter. "There's no other alternative."

More than just the frantic pace of the cause bothered Chavez. Lately, many farm workers had raised the notion of using violence as a weapon in the strike. Already, some farm workers had committed crimes. Filipino farm worker Alfonso Pereira was sentenced to a year in jail after trying to run down three growers in his car. In addition, the Kern County district attorney's office announced an investigation into vandalism allegedly committed by union members on farm properties.

Chavez was alarmed at the rising tide of violence in the union. He was a man, after all, who followed the principles of Mohandas Gandhi and Martin Luther King, Jr. Elsewhere, it was hard to ignore that social activism in America often got out of hand. The civil rights movement, for example, had often turned violent. In fact, members of the radical Black Panther Party urged violence as a tool for social change. Later that year, violence would erupt on the streets of Chicago when thousands of anti-war demonstrators clashed with police while protesting at the Democratic National Convention. Indeed, the year would turn even more violent. King and Robert Kennedy would both be murdered by assassins.

Chavez wanted no part of violence. Angered, he called United Farm Workers leaders together and barked at them, "We'll never be able to get anywhere if we start using tactics of violence. You have to believe in that!"

Chavez sought a way to drive his message home to the farm workers. Finally, he turned to the writings of Gandhi who had often fasted for the cause of Indian independence. The union leader decided his fast would be "an act of penance, recalling workers to the nonviolent roots of their movement."

He commenced the fast on February 15, resolving to

consume only water. At first, he kept the fast private but after four days, Chavez convened a meeting of union leaders and announced that he would not take another bite of food until every member of the United Farm Workers made a pledge to nonviolence.

"Cesar took a very hard line," said Leroy Chatfield, a union leader. "We were falling back on violence because we weren't creative enough to find another solution, because we didn't work hard enough. One of the things that he said in the speech was that he felt we had lost our will to win, by which he meant that acting violently or advocating violence or even thinking that maybe violence wasn't such a bad thing—that is really losing your will to win, your commitment to win. A cop-out. This seems like a very idealistic position, but there's truth in it.

ROBERT F. KENNEDY

Robert F. Kennedy was one of nine children of Joseph and Rose Kennedy, a wealthy and politically influential Massachusetts couple. Joseph Kennedy served as an ambassador to Great Britain. Robert Kennedy's older brother, John F. Kennedy, was elected president of the United States in 1960.

Born in 1925, "Bobby" Kennedy served as attorney general in his brother's administration. Following the assassination of John F. Kennedy in 1963, Bobby Kennedy won election to the U.S. Senate, representing New York State. In 1968, he ran for president himself. He won Democratic primaries in Indiana, Nebraska and California. On the night of June 5, 1968, just after speaking at a celebration marking his victory in California, Kennedy was assassinated by gunman Sirhan Sirhan while leaving a crowded hotel ballroom through a kitchen.

Kennedy had often pledged his support to the United Farm Workers. Cesar Chavez and Dolores Huerta were both in the ballroom that night and had personally congratulated Kennedy on his victory just moments before the shooting.

Anarchy leads to chaos, and out of chaos rises the demagogue."

There was considerable dissent in the top ranks of the union leadership over the fast. Some leaders quit the union, arguing that Chavez was setting himself up as an icon, trying to convince people that he had mythical powers that would see him through the ordeal. By and large, though, most members of the union supported their leader. When Chavez arrived at a court appearance in Bakersfield to defend the union against a charge of improper picketing, more than 3,000 farm workers met him at the courthouse and knelt down in prayer.

Chavez spent most of his time during the fast at Forty Acres, a former migrant labor camp near Delano that the union had converted into its headquarters. Chavez lived in a hut on the campgrounds. He slept on a cot and spent his days reading and praying.

Soon, Forty Acres became the epicenter of the strike. Each day, hundreds of farm workers would arrive at the camp to greet Chavez, show support for their president and present him with small gifts—usually crucifixes or other religious symbols. The news media flooded into Delano as well. Quickly, the story of Chavez's fast found its way onto the front pages as well as the nightly national newscasts.

Through it all, Chavez insisted that the fast had but one purpose—to discourage violence by union members.

"If the strike means the blood of one grower or one grower's son, or one worker or one worker's son, then it isn't worth it," Chavez said.

By early March, the union's rank and file had embraced Chavez's message. Chavez had, of course, grown weak during the fast. Weighing 175 pounds before he gave up food, Chavez lost more than 30 pounds during his hunger strike. For years, a sore back had bothered Chavez. The lack of food inflamed the injury, making it even more painful.

And so Chavez announced that he would end the hunger strike on March 11 after 25 days of subsisting on just water.

Dolores Huerta, for one, believed the fast served its purpose. She said, "Prior to the fast there had been a lot of bickering and backbiting and fighting, and little attempts at violence. But Cesar brought everybody together and really established himself as a leader of the farm workers."

More than 6,000 farm workers gathered in a Delano park on March 11 to witness a ceremony ending the fast. Senator Robert Kennedy, who would announce his presidential campaign just a few days later, flew in to be part of the celebration. During the fast, Kennedy sent a telegram to Chavez endorsing the hunger strike. "Your work and your belief have always been based solely on principles of non-violence," Kennedy wrote. "You have my best wishes and my deepest concern in these difficult hours."

When the two men met in the Delano park, they broke bread together and each took a bite. Meanwhile, loaves of bread were passed through the crowd and thousands of farm workers joined Kennedy and Chavez in the ritual. Kennedy spoke to the crowd, calling Chavez "one of the heroic figures of our time." Chavez had prepared a speech but he was too weak to deliver it. Others read the speech for him.

"It is how we use our lives that determines what kind of men we are," the speech said. "The strongest act of manliness is to sacrifice ourselves for others in a totally nonviolent struggle for justice. To be a man is to suffer for others. God help us be men."

Chavez's fast got the farm workers back on the right track. Nevertheless, the growers still refused to recognize the union even though the boycott was beginning to affect them economically. By August 1968, the California grape growers reported that sales had fallen by some 20 percent. The reduced demand for table grapes caused prices to drop by about 15 percent during the first year of the strike. A year later, the growers reported that the boycott had cost them $25 million.

By 1970, 10 growers in the Coachella Valley north of

U.S. Senator Robert Kennedy and Chavez break bread in March 1968, effectively ending the 25-day fast Chavez undertook to support the United Farm Workers strike against grape growers, and to demonstrate that non-violent means of protest were a powerful means of championing the cause of farm workers' rights. Kennedy endorsed Chavez's hunger strike and praised Chavez for his nonviolent principles.

Borrego Springs announced their willingness to recognize the United Farm Workers and negotiate a contract. This was the first crack. The Coachella growers were responsible for just 15 percent of the California grape crop. Nevertheless, their five-year-old united front finally collapsed. In the coming months, other growers would agree to contracts as well.

And then, on July 25, 1970, representatives from Giumarra Vineyards contacted attorneys for the United Farm Workers and said the company was willing to talk about a contract. Hours later, Chavez and United Farm Workers attorney Jerry Cohen met with company owners John Giumarra, Sr. and John Giumarra, Jr. in a motel room outside Delano.

The negotiations over the Giumarra contract went quickly, but Chavez had a significant demand. He knew the Giumarras were influential in the California farm industry, and he wanted them to convince the 28 other growers who had not yet given in to settle as well.

"We wanted them to round up all the growers," Cohen said. "They said they could do it."

Four days later, the Giumarras as well as representatives of most of the other growers gathered at Forty Acres to sign contracts with the United Farm Workers. The contracts guaranteed the workers salaries of $1.80 an hour—as much as $0.80 an hour more than they had earned when the strike began. The growers agreed to set up committees that would include union representatives to monitor pesticide use on the farms. The use of pesticides had long concerned union leaders who believed the chemicals could be affecting the health of the workers. Other benefits included in the contract were bonuses for extra work and an employer contribution to an employee health plan.

Perhaps the most significant concession by the growers was to permit the union to run hiring halls. Traditionally, the growers had hired their own workers or turned to labor contractors to supply pickers. The workers were usually bused to the farms for their days' employment from migrant camps or pickup points in nearby towns. Often, the Mexicans called the pickup point *El Hoyo*, which means "The Hole." The hiring halls meant the workers would report first to union headquarters and that a union official would then dispatch the

John Giumarra, Jr., a grape grower in California, holds up the label of the United Farm Workers as Chavez (left) applauds. Once the boycott attained the cooperation of Giumarra Vineyards, the solidarity of the growers cracked, and many began negotiating with the union.

workers to the farms that needed labor. Hiring halls had been used for decades in many unions, particularly in the building trades, that find jobs for carpenters, electricians, plumbers, roofers and other tradesmen.

By controlling the hiring halls, the United Farm Workers could make sure that only its members would find jobs on the farms. And that meant the growers could not turn to illegal immigrant labor to work in their fields.

The contracts with the grape growers proved that farm workers could remain united through a long and bitter strike. That unity would be tested again quite soon. As Cesar Chavez and other United Farm Workers leaders were soon to learn, the shadow of the Teamsters Union would once again fall across the farm fields of California.

6

Stealing the Fruit

The ink had barely dried on the contracts with the grape growers when Cesar Chavez learned of trouble elsewhere. In central California's Salinas Valley, lettuce growers signed contracts with the Teamsters, designating the rival union as the official bargaining agent for their workers. Chavez hurried to the town of Salinas, not knowing that he was embarking on a disastrous confrontation with the Teamsters that would lead to bloodshed as well as the near destruction of the United Farm Workers.

The lettuce growers watched the long boycott against grapes unfold with a sense of horror. Fearing that Chavez would declare a similar boycott against them when the grape growers finally caved in, the lettuce farmers sought out the Teamsters, which they believed would be a more cooperative organization. By then, most of the growers realized it would be futile to try to keep the unions off their fields. Most growers regarded Chavez as a hothead who resorted to such theatrical tactics as a hunger strike, the *Perigrinacion* or the boycott.

Cesar Chavez speaks at a rally in Salinas, California, to launch a nationwide boycott of non-union lettuce. He began this campaign directly on the heels of his success with the grape industry.

Why not deal with a union that would make far fewer demands at the bargaining table? Indeed, the Teamsters had already agreed that it would not maintain hiring halls—meaning the growers, not the union, would retain the power to recruit workers.

"The grape boycott scared the heck out of the farmers, all of us," said lettuce grower Daryl Arnold. "The (growers) felt that the Teamsters were the best organization to represent the farm workers in the area. . . . They thought if they could sign a contract with (them) it would forestall Cesar trying to come in and take over the industry."

By the time Chavez arrived in Salinas, 30 growers had signed contracts with the Teamsters and another 175 were in negotiations. Quickly, Chavez established a union headquarters in Salinas and distributed election cards to farm workers, imploring them to designate the United Farm Workers as their union. Chavez was certain that the Teamsters did not have the support of a majority of farm workers in the Salinas Valley.

There were plenty of indications that he was correct. Two thousand farm workers marched into a college football stadium in Salinas for a United Farm Workers rally on August 2, 1970. Chanting *"Huelga! Huelga!"* repeatedly, the farm workers cheered wildly as Chavez strode out to the middle of the football field to address them.

"It's tragic that these men have not yet come to understand that we are in a new age, a new era," Chavez told the farm workers. "No longer can a couple of white men sit together and write the destinies of all the Chicanos and Filipinos in this valley."

It was true that at the time of the Salinas rally, the Teamsters had signed up few farm workers. But that was soon to change. Teamsters organizers were dispatched into the farm fields, and this time they resolved not to make the same mistakes they made in their first farm workers union effort in 1966. Teamsters leaders poured $100,000 a month into the farm workers' membership drive. They had membership cards, as well as fliers outlining their proposals, printed in Spanish, promising steadier work than the United Farm Workers could deliver. Very shortly, farm workers started signing up with the other union. The growers fired many farm workers who refused to sign with the Teamsters.

The United Farm Workers responded by calling a strike and throwing up a picket line against Fresh Pict, a corporation that owned a Salinas lettuce farm that fired about 100 farm workers who refused to join the Teamsters. Farm workers on a nearby strawberry farm owned by Pic N Pac, another corporate owner, walked off their jobs in solidarity with the lettuce pickers.

A volunteer on a New York City subway hands out information about the lettuce boycott that Chavez organized in 1973. Unlike his previous efforts against the grape growers, Chavez could never muster the same public support against the lettuce growers.

Fresh Pict responded by obtaining a court injunction forbidding picketing in front of its properties. In defiance of the order, Chavez himself showed up in front of the Fresh Pict office to carry a picket sign.

The United Farm Workers were taking other steps as well. Chavez was not sure a lettuce boycott would be effective; unlike grapes, lettuce was a staple on most American tables. He believed people might be hesitant to give up lettuce. Instead, he sent word to United Fruit Company, which owned lettuce farms in Salinas, that the union was ready to call for a boycott of the company's bananas, which were grown in Central American countries. That threat got United Fruit's attention. Executives from the company agreed to meet with the United Farm Workers to talk about a settlement, which Chavez insisted should include a dismissal of the Teamsters contracts. Fresh Pict executives joined the talks as well.

Meanwhile, the Teamsters found trouble in the fields. The union had signed contracts with lettuce growers that guaranteed their members just a token increase in wages over the five-year term of the pacts. When many of the lettuce pickers learned of the new wage scale, they became enraged. They met in hastily called meetings and vowed to strike. Chavez sent representatives to the meetings, urging the lettuce pickers to stay calm and put their faith in the United Farm Workers who were trying to negotiate new deals with the lettuce growers. The pickers went back to work, agreeing to wait.

Chavez's negotiations with Fresh Pict and United Fruit ended suddenly when several of the other lettuce growers announced that they intended to observe the terms of their Teamsters contracts. A strike was inevitable. On August 23, farm workers again rallied in the Salinas football stadium and pledged to strike. More than 10,000 of them would walk off their jobs within the next few days. As for Chavez, he had no choice but to call for a nationwide lettuce boycott.

Not only were the United Farm Workers opposing the growers, but they had also made enemies of the Teamsters that supported the strike against the grape growers and helped with the national grape boycott as well. The two sides quickly came to blows. Once again, Chavez admonished his union members to adhere to a strict policy of nonviolence, but the Teamsters, whose members reveled in their two-fisted reputation, made no such commitment. One of the first United Farm Workers members to be injured was Jerry Cohen, the union attorney, who was hospitalized with a concussion after a picket-line scuffle with Teamsters. Other violent acts occurred, some committed by United Farm Workers members.

Unlike the grape strike, which lasted five years, the lettuce strike soon started to pay dividends. In September, Fresh Pict and Pic N Pac agreed to drop the Teamsters contracts and recognize the United Farm Workers. Chavez's union also negotiated a contract with lettuce grower InterHarvest, giving workers the unheard of wage of $2.10 an hour—$0.50 an hour more than the minimum wage at the time.

Nevertheless, other growers refused to drop their Teamsters deals. Bud Antle Company, a Salinas corporate grower, insisted on maintaining its Teamsters agreement. Chavez responded by calling for a boycott of Bud Antle lettuce. The company won a court order declaring the boycott illegal. Chavez insisted that the boycott would continue. On December 10, he was jailed by a judge in Salinas for refusing to abide by the court order. He remained in jail until December 24, when he was released after union attorneys filed an appeal with a higher court. While in prison, he was visited by Ethel Kennedy, the widow of slain presidential candidate Robert F. Kennedy, and Coretta Scott King, widow of assassinated civil rights leader Martin Luther King, Jr. Eventually, the California Supreme Court ruled that the injunction banning the boycott was illegal.

For a time, it appeared the United Farm Workers had weathered the challenge posed by the Teamsters. The lettuce growers proved far less resilient than the grape growers. It was true that many growers still refused to negotiate, but others had caved in rather than risk losing business because of the boycott. Only nonunion California growers were subjected to the boycott. Consumers were told to look for the "union bug" on lettuce packaging. The union bug is the tiny symbol found on a label that indicates the product was manufactured with union labor. During the United Farm Workers' boycotts, consumers were asked to look for a tiny facsimile of the union's black Aztec eagle printed on the packaging.

If Chavez and other United Farm Workers leaders believed they had won the battle for the hearts and minds of the public, they were wrong. In 1973, the three-year-old grape growers' contracts expired. Instead of bargaining again with Chavez, the growers signed contracts with the Teamsters. Other growers signed with the Teamsters as well. At the start of 1973, the United Farm Workers held contracts with about 300 growers. Within a year, they had lost all but a dozen of those contracts, representing fewer than 5,000 workers. By early 1974, the Teamsters won contracts with more than 350 growers, representing 55,000 workers in California and Arizona.

Chavez saw the collapse of his union and lamented, "We shook the tree and now the Teamsters are stealing the fruit."

The Teamsters had managed to win support by returning to their aggressive tactics, promising laborers more than the United Farm Workers could honestly deliver. Sympathetic police departments helped the Teamsters where they could, pushing United Farm Workers organizers away from farm entrances.

Reporters lost interest in the United Farm Workers. Rallies, pickets and other demonstrations ceased being news, probably because there was really so little new about them. After all, Chavez's union had been on strike in one form or another since 1965; by 1974 other stories were dominating the headlines.

One of those stories was inflation. During the 1970s, the price of oil suddenly shot skyward. With gasoline costing much more, prices for nearly everything else shot up as well. If it cost twice as much for gasoline to ship truckloads of lettuce across country, the consumer was bound to see that increase in the cost of a head of lettuce. Consequently, consumers became more concerned with the cost of a head of lettuce rather than who had picked it and at what wage.

Violence continued to erupt in the fields. On August 13, 1973, a group of farm workers congregated on a Fresno street corner to celebrate the release of union members who had been imprisoned on illegal picketing charges for several weeks. Police arrived and ordered the farm workers to disperse. Words were exchanged and soon the two sides were scuffling. During the melee, a policeman swinging a flashlight struck Nagi Daifullah, a 24-year-old farm worker from Yemen, on the head. He

The widow of slain striker Juan de la Cruz places a flower on his casket, as Chavez (center) pays his respects. Cruz died when violence erupted between United Farm Workers and Teamsters. The Teamsters developed a reputation for sometimes using violent methods to get what they wanted.

collapsed, hitting his head on the concrete as he fell to the ground. Daifullah died the next day.

Two days later, United Farm Worker Juan de la Cruz was picketing in Kern County when he stepped out of line for a drink of water. Suddenly, a car sped by the picketers. Witnesses saw a rifle barrel poke out of a car window. A shot exploded, striking De la Cruz in the chest. The 60-year-old farm worker died in a hospital the next day.

"After people started to get killed, there was a visible change in Cesar," said Luis Valdez, leader of the *Teatro Campesino* theatrical troupe. "He felt personally responsible—I mean that in every sense of the word—personally responsible for the life and death of the people in the union."

At Teamsters headquarters in Washington, union officials had nothing but disdain for Chavez. When Teamsters President Frank Fitzsimmons was questioned by reporters on the fairness of his union's assault on the United Farm Workers, he angrily replied, "Why don't you guys ask Chavez about how he gets out of his Lincoln limousine a mile away and how he changes from his tuxedo into work pants when he goes visiting the farm workers."

By the end of 1973, roughly 3,500 farm workers had been arrested for violating injunctions barring picketing at nonunion or Teamster farm fields. By then, Chavez had called for boycotts on grapes and lettuce that did not carry the Aztec eagle symbol as well as the beverages sold by the Ernest & Julio Gallo Wine Company. That firm, a huge California winemaker, had also rejected negotiations with the United Farm Workers in favor of doing business with the Teamsters. Chavez insisted that the Teamsters did not have the support of the workers, but company co-owner Ernest Gallo disagreed.

"Because we have honored the wishes of our farm workers to change unions we have been caught in a jurisdictional dispute between two unions," he said.

Throughout the early 1970s, it had become clear to Chavez that there were few laws on the books in California governing the activities of farm workers or their rights to bargain collectively and strike. True, there was federal law—the National Labor Relations Act—that gave all workers in America the right to join unions. But Chavez felt farm workers faced obstacles that were not covered by federal law. Most spoke little English or no English at all, for example. Most farm workers continued to live as migrants, traveling from farm to farm, harvest to harvest.

Chavez believed California needed its own farm labor law that would include protections for the migrants as well as the union organizers who were all too vulnerable to strong-arm tactics employed by the growers and rival unions. Chavez also wanted a law that would prevent growers from negotiating with unions, such as the Teamsters, that had not been legitimately selected for representation by the workers. Finally, Chavez wanted the law to permit the union to call for public boycotts. In 1971, the conservative state government in Arizona outlawed union-sponsored boycotts, and Chavez was concerned other state governments would follow Arizona's lead. Chavez began calling for a comprehensive California farm labor law.

Until 1975, though, such a law had little chance of adoption in California. The governor of California was Ronald Reagan, a conservative Republican who was no friend of organized labor. Indeed, after taking office as president in 1981, Reagan fired all air traffic controllers employed by the federal government because he believed they had staged an illegal strike.

The mood in Sacramento changed in 1975 when Governor Jerry Brown took office. The son of former Governor Pat Brown,

JERRY BROWN

Edmund G. "Jerry" Brown, Jr. was born in 1938 and grew up the son Governor Pat Brown. After obtaining his law degree from Yale University, Brown followed his father into California politics, winning elections first as secretary of state and then, in 1974, as governor.

In addition to establishing the first agricultural labor relations law in the nation, Brown's tenure as governor included measures to protect California's environment. He started the California Conservation Corps, signed the California Coastal Protection Act into law, opposed expansion of the nuclear power industry and encouraged Californians to conserve energy and employ alternative energy sources, such as solar power.

Brown ran for president of the United States in 1976 and 1992. At the 1976 Democratic National Convention in New York City, Cesar Chavez placed Brown's name in nomination. Brown never became president, but he refused to retire from public life. In 1998, Brown was elected mayor of Oakland, California. He was reelected in 2002.

Actors Edward James Olmos (left, in red cap) and Martin Sheen (center) march with thousands of United Farm Workers supporters. The walk commemorated the 40th anniversary of the union and celebrated Cesar Chavez's involvement with the union and its activities.

Jerry Brown had a far different political philosophy than the anti-union conservatism espoused by Reagan. A liberal Democrat, Brown had long supported the United Farm Workers. In 1972, Brown—who was then California's secretary of state—opposed a referendum backed by the growers to outlaw union-backed boycotts. Brown, whose department administered elections, uncovered fraud in the growers' campaign, and the referendum was eventually defeated at the polls.

In 1975, as governor, he welcomed the opportunity to hammer out a farm labor law. It took several months of negotiations involving Brown and his aides as well as Chavez and other Farm Workers Union leaders. Influential members of the California Legislature had to be consulted as well. The Teamsters and growers fought hard against the law, lobbying legislators to turn down the measure. Finally, on June 5, 1975, Brown announced that a law protecting the rights of farm workers had been forged. The state's Agricultural Labor Relations Act was adopted by the State Assembly and signed into law by Brown.

A board was established by the law to oversee working conditions for farm laborers. Under the legislation, the board included membership by farm workers. Field offices were established throughout the state. They served as bases for inspectors who traveled from farm to farm, making sure working conditions were acceptable, wages were paid and legal union activity was permitted. When the United Farm Workers received complaints from their members about abuses or violations of the law, the act contained a provision for the filing of formal complaints. In fact, during the first two months the law was in effect, the United Farm Workers filed more than 1,000 complaints.

The law clearly had an impact. By the middle of 1976, workers on more than 80 farms had voted to join unions, and the clear majority of them elected to join the United Farm Workers. Membership of Chavez's union ballooned to roughly 22,000 workers.

As for the Teamsters, the union soon lost interest in organizing farm workers.

Death of the Fighter

Cesar Chavez spent the night of April 22, 1993, in a hotel room in Yuma, Arizona, preparing to defend in court the United Farm Workers against a lawsuit filed by Bruce Church Inc., one of the world's largest lettuce growers. The lawsuit had been filed nine years before, alleging that union pickets in front of supermarkets hurt Bruce Church's sales. Since Arizona's laws were much more sympathetic to the growers, the company elected to file the lawsuit in that state.

There was a certain amount of irony involved in the case. Bruce Church had eventually become the owner of the farm the Chavez family was forced to leave in 1937.

Chavez would never testify in the Bruce Church case. That night, he died quietly in his sleep. He was 66 years old.

For Chavez, adoption of California's Agricultural Labor Relations Act represented a single tiny victory in the ongoing struggle to win rights and fair wages for farm workers. Soon after

Chavez continued to be a spokesman for farm workers and their pursuit of fair working conditions into his later years. The night he died, Chavez was preparing for a court case concerning the United Farm Worker's involvement in a strike against a lettuce grower.

the law was passed, pro-grower legislators in the California Assembly found a way to strip the Agricultural Labor Relations Board of many of its powers by reducing its budget. In 1976, the union backed adoption of California Proposition 14, a referendum that would have compelled legislators to fully fund the board. However, the ballot question failed at the polls after the growers mounted a well-funded campaign to defeat it.

Meanwhile, the Teamsters made their peace with the United Farm Workers, officially signing an agreement in 1977 that ensured the rival union would never again attempt to organize farm workers.

Governor Jerry Brown won re-election in 1978, but in 1982 he was replaced by Governor George Deukmejian, a Republican whose campaign received more than $1 million in support from the growers. Deukemejian was far less sympathetic to the farm workers' plight than Brown; soon after entering office, he began stripping the Agricultural Labor Relations Board of its already-thin budgets and many of its staff members. He closed several of the board's offices around the state, depriving farm workers of places where they could file complaints against growers.

Emboldened by the state government's support, the growers stepped up their anti-union activities. Growers fired union members and refused to speak with United Farm Workers representatives. On many farms, where union organizing persisted, hostilities between the two sides often flared up. In September 1983, United Farm Workers organizer Rene Lopez was shot to death at a migrant labor camp near Fresno by a guard working for a grower.

"Rene is gone because he dared to hope and because he dared to live out his hopes," Chavez said at Lopez's funeral. "It was not possible to shut his eyes to situations of distress and poverty, which cry out to God, or to keep silent in the face of injustice. How many more farm workers must fall? How many more martyrs must there be before we can be free?"

Throughout the 1980s and early 1990s, Chavez employed the same tactics the union had used since the 1960s. He led union members on long marches that culminated in rallies in

Farm workers protest the use of pesticides on produce and the vulnerability of the workers' health. Chavez (second man on the left) fasted for 36 days in 1988 to support the United Farm Workers' anti-pesticides stance, but the union would have little success stopping the industry's use of the poisons.

front of the seats of government or the corporate offices of growers. He went on hunger strikes. He called for boycotts of grapes, lettuce and other farm commodities. He led walkouts. The tactics had mixed results. In 1988, his 36-day fast to protest the use of farm pesticides and their effects on the health of workers called attention to the issue, but growers persisted in their use. In 2001, the California Cancer Registry, a state agency that collects data on cancer cases, released a study reporting that Hispanic farm workers have higher rates of leukemia as well as brain, skin and stomach cancers than Hispanics who do not work in farm fields.

"The union's position is that it's directly related to pesticide use," declared Douglas Blaylock, administrator of the United Farm Workers' medical plan.

Even at farms where pesticides are not used, abuses of workers' rights are often reported. During the 1980s and 1990s, many farms turned to "organic" agriculture—a process in which no pesticides or herbicides are used. Many health-conscious consumers demand products untouched by chemicals and are willing to pay a premium to get them. Indeed, some stores sell only organic produce.

But many of the organic farms have had little regard for workers' rights. In Oregon, 34 farm workers sued Willamette River Organics, owner of one of the largest organic farms in the state, alleging that they were cheated by supervisors who undercounted their bushels and that anyone asking for a break was threatened with dismissal.

Elsewhere, other abuses were uncovered. Arizona authorities uncovered squalid living conditions for farm workers at an organic farm in that state where children under the age of 14 were employed in the fields and supervisors threatened to shoot workers who complained.

Although the workers would not have to worry about health issues stemming from pesticide use on organic farms, organic crops offered their own problems to the farm workers. On organic farms, crops need much more individual attention. Since herbicides are not employed to keep weed growth down, farm workers have to spend much more time pulling weeds from the fields. By then, most states had outlawed the notorious short hoe, but on organic farms growers refused to issue long hoes to the workers, believing the large tools would damage the crops. Instead, most workers on organic farms were sent into the fields with no tools at all and told to pull weeds by hand.

Abuses of farm workers' rights have not been limited to organic farms. By the year 2000 in California, the minimum wage had risen to $6.25 an hour, but many farm workers were lucky to get half that.

By then, most growers turned to farm labor contractors to provide the laborers for their fields. By 2001, around 1,200 contractors were in business in the state.

The U.S. Immigration and Naturalization Service, which is responsible for apprehending illegal immigrants and returning them to their home countries, found that many of California's farm labor contractors made deals with "coyotes"—smugglers who sneak aliens across the border from Mexico, then bus them to the California farm fields.

The contractors are responsible for paying the workers, and they find it easy to cheat the illegal aliens. Meanwhile, the growers know there is keen competition for the labor contracts, so they force the contractors to bid low for the jobs. It all means the farm worker is abused.

"A man works an eight-hour day and they only pay him $40. But they report only five hours. It looks like the man made $8 an hour. It's crooked, it's dirty and I don't do that," said Larry Peters, vice president of a farm labor contracting firm that refuses to use illegal aliens.

In 1998, the U.S. Labor Department conducted inspections at 66 farms in the San Joaquin, Coachella and Napa valleys. It found pickers were earning less than the minimum wage at a third of the grape farms in those valleys.

Workers have been abused in other ways. For example, labor contractors usually have to provide buses to transport workers to farms, sometimes dozens of miles away. Many workers had to endure bus rides of two hours or more before they arrived at their jobs. But the labor contractors refused

Arturo Rodriguez became president of the United Farm Workers after Chavez's death in 1993. One of his first triumphs as president, a positive sign for the future of the union, was the contract negotiation with strawberry growers.

to pay them for the travel time, insisting that they could earn money only for the time they spent in the fields. Finally, in 2000, the California Supreme Court ruled that workers' "compulsory travel time" had to be compensated by the farm labor contractors.

Throughout this era, the United Farm Workers did what it could to fight for workers' rights. After the death of Cesar

Chavez, Arturo Rodriguez became union president. Rodriguez, who married Chavez's daughter Linda, served as Cesar's right hand for years as union vice president. After a long fight in 2000, the union won a contract with Coastal Berry Company, which grows strawberries on roughly 1,000 acres in Ventura County, California. The contract ensured some workers would receive as much as $10 an hour. It also established health and dental benefits for farm workers.

The strawberry growers had been among the last group of farmers in California to resist union efforts. Many strawberry

ARTURO RODRIGUEZ

Arturo Rodriguez does not fit the profile of the typical farm worker. Born in Texas, Rodriguez earned a college degree and was studying for a master's degree in social work at the University of Michigan in 1973. It was there, while helping organize a grape boycott on campus, that Rodriguez met Linda Chavez, Cesar Chavez's daughter. The two were married in 1974.

Cesar Chavez soon recognized the leadership qualities in his son-in-law and dispatched Rodriguez to help lead many of the union's organizing activities. He was eventually named a vice president of the United Farm Workers. Following Chavez's death in 1993, Rodriguez was elected president of the union. He is regarded as a shrewd negotiator who commands the respect of his adversaries and peers. After he was elected United Farm Workers president, he was awarded a seat on the National Labor Council, the policy-making body of the AFL-CIO, the nation's largest union.

"You know, you work around Cesar for years and years and years, and you're part of a movement, but you never really appreciate the full impact of what he did, and the sacrifice he went through, and the work he did all these years, until you get in the position I'm in now," Rodriguez said shortly after his election as union president.

growers would plow under their crops rather than negotiate with the United Farm Workers. The contract with Coastal Berry was, therefore, a major breakthrough for the union. Also, the United Farm Workers finally made peace with the grape growers. After a group of grape growers agreed to union contracts in 2000, Rodriguez officially called off the grape boycott. It had been declared on and off by Chavez since the days of the Delano strike in 1968.

Clearly, though, the final years of the grape boycott had gone virtually unnoticed by the public. "The bottom line is that it never worked. It wasn't effective," said Bob Krauter, a spokesman for the California Farm Bureau Federation, an organization of growers. "The union just had to have something to say when they called it off."

The union gained one of its final victories in August 2001 when California Governor Gray Davis signed a law cracking down on farm labor contractors who cheat their workers. Under the law, labor contractors could face fines of as much as $25,000 if they are found to be cheating their workers. The union sought the law because of the failure of the old Agricultural Labor Relations Board to pursue violators. The new statute would enable law enforcement officials, such as district attorneys, to arrest unscrupulous labor contractors.

"The state inspection system simply hasn't worked," said Marc Grossman, a spokesman for the United Farm Workers. "The record is pretty dismal under Democratic and Republican administrations. We're hoping that elected district attorneys respond to this because Latinos are increasingly more influential in local politics and at the ballot box."

The union eventually changed its name to the United Farm Workers of America, but the organization was never able to grow into the national union Cesar Chavez envisioned when he first walked into the farm fields in 1962. The influence of the union rarely spread outside California, and inside the state it has consistently found it difficult to maintain membership. In the twenty-first century, the union has found itself dealing with the same difficulties every union that has tried to organize farm laborers has found: workers migrate from farm to farm, following the harvest. Rarely do the majority of them remain in one place long enough to put down roots, establish a community and join a union that will stand up for their rights. Despite winning a string of union elections on farm fields in 2000, the United Farm Workers could report a dues-paying membership of just 27,000 farm workers out of the more than 500,000 farm workers believed to be employed in the California fields.

Cesar Chavez was buried in Delano on April 29, 1993. He was buried in a simple pine box that was built by his brother, Richard. Throughout his life, Chavez had never sought wealth, fame or political power for himself. In death, he wished to have a simple funeral.

Nevertheless, more than 40,000 mourners made their way to the tiny California town where the union he founded had scored its greatest victory. Jerry Brown and Ethel Kennedy attended the funeral. Mickey Kantor, a high-ranking member of the administration of President Bill Clinton, had once served as a United Farm Workers lawyer and attended the funeral as well. Hundreds of people marched in a procession as Chavez's casket was carried through the streets of Delano.

"Cesar wasn't afraid of anybody," Brown said at the funeral. "He was a real fighter. The farmers were scared to death of him. I remember the first time I saw him. He walked into my father's house . . . and he was dressed the same way as when I saw him a month ago. He never lost his modesty and simplicity."

It is likely that Chavez would have been greatly embarrassed if he had known he would be at the center of all that attention. For years, he battled against the perception that he was a mythical figure among farm workers—that his presence was accompanied by a certain mystique.

"I don't think it's a mystique," he once told a reporter. "It's a matter of friendships, of knowing the workers and of being

Jerry Brown, seen here campaigning in his bid to become governor of California, was an early Chavez supporter. Chavez's ability to win the respect, admiration and support of his fellow farm workers, the general public and politicians alike, is a testament to his great powers as a leader and transformer of society.

with them. I was the first member of the union. I organized it. I consider myself more an organizer than a leader—though it's impossible for me to tell you how I make that distinction. But I do. In the beginning it was just an awful lot of hard work and planning and plodding. I was scared when I tried to speak at my first meeting. Awfully scared. But eventually, I learned. And I met an awful lot of workers. I know thousands of them, personally. So a lot of things happen because of friendship, not because of any mystique, or secret power of personality or any of that stuff. It's all very flattering, but it's not true."

Chronology

1927   Cesar Chavez is born on his family's farm outside Yuma, Arizona.

1935   Journalist Robert Geiger calls the drought-ravaged farm lands of the plains states the "Dust Bowl."

1937   The Chavez family loses their farm and are forced to become migrant farm workers.

1939   John Steinbeck publishes *The Grapes of Wrath*, a novel that tells of the plight of migrant farm workers.

1940   Saul Alinsky founds the Industrial Area Foundation; the social activist eventually becomes a mentor to Chavez.

1943   Mexican Americans are injured and their homes and businesses are vandalized by whites in Los Angeles during the "Zoot Suit Riots."

1947   A 20-month strike staged by the National Farm Labor Union commences against DiGiorgio Fruit Corporation; the strike ultimately fails to win bargaining power for the union.

1952   Chavez joins the Community Service Organization, a group under the umbrella of Alinsky's Industrial Area Foundation.

1962   Chavez resigns from the Community Service Organization to found a farm workers' union.

1964   The Federal law permitting importation of cheap Mexican laborers known as *braceros* expires.

1965   Under Chavez's leadership, the National Farm Workers of America joins with the Agricultural Workers Organizing Committee to declare a strike on grape growers.

1966   The National Farm Workers of America merges with the Agricultural Workers Organizing Committee, forming the United Farm Workers. Chavez leads a 300-mile march from Delano to Sacramento known as the *Perigrinacion*; he then reaches settlement with California wineries on farm workers' contract demands.

1968 Chavez calls for a national boycott on table grapes and fasts for 25 days to discourage violence by striking farm workers.

1970 The strike against grape growers ends when the growers agree to recognize the United Farm Workers and raise wages for farm laborers. Meanwhile, lettuce growers sign contracts with the Teamsters to head off plans by Chavez's union to organize lettuce pickers. Chavez is jailed for 14 days for refusing to abide by a court order barring a lettuce boycott.

1973 Grape growers sign new contracts with the Teamsters. United Farm Workers membership falls to 5,000 workers. Two union members lose their lives in violent confrontations.

1975 California adopts the Agricultural Labor Relations Act, guaranteeing rights for farm workers.

1977 The Teamsters officially drop efforts to organize farm workers.

1982 California Governor George Deukmejian reduces the budget for the Agricultural Labor Relations Board, closing many of its offices and making it hard for farm workers to file complaints.

1988 Chavez fasts for 36 days to protest use of pesticides on farms.

1993 Chavez dies in Yuma, Arizona; his son-in-law, Arturo Rodriguez, is named president of the union.

2000 Strawberry growers sign their first contracts with the United Farm Workers.

Bibliography

Baca, Kim. "Study: Farmworkers Experience Higher Rates of Leukemia, Brain, Prostate, Skin Cancers." The Associated Press, March 17, 2002.

Ballad, Richard. "Penthouse Interview: Cesar Chavez." *Penthouse*, July 1975.

Brill, Steven. *The Teamsters*. New York: Simon and Schuster, 1978.

Chavez, Cesar. "Sharing the Wealth." *Playboy*, January 1970.

De Toledano, Ralph. *Little Cesar*. Washington, D.C.: Anthem Books, 1971.

Dunne, John Gregory. *Delano: The Story of the California Grape Strike*. New York: Farrar, Straus and Giroux, 1967.

Ferriss, Susan, and Ricardo Sandoval. *The Fight in the Fields: Cesar Chavez and the Farmworkers Movement*. New York: Harcourt Brace and Company, 1997.

Furillo, Andy. "Dirt Cheap." *The Sacramento Bee*, May 20-22, 2001.

Galaraza, Ernesto. *Farm Workers and Agri-business in California, 1947-1960*. South Bend, Indiana: University of Notre Dame Press, 1977.

Griffith, Winthrop. "Is Chavez Beaten?" *The New York Times Sunday Magazine*, September 15, 1974.

Lindsey, Robert. "Cesar Chavez, 66, Organizer of Union for Migrants, Dies." *The New York Times*, April 2, 1993.

Matthiessen, Peter. *Sal Si Puedes: Cesar Chavez and the New American Revolution*. New York: Random House, 1969.

Maxwell, Lesli A. "Davis OKs Law on Farm Wages." *The Fresno Bee*, August 10, 2001.

Rainey, James. "Farm Workers Union Ends 16-Year Boycott of Grapes." *Los Angeles Times*, November 22, 2000.

Roane, Kit R. "Ripe for Abuse." *U.S. News and World Report,* April 22, 2002.

Rodebaugh, Dale. "UFW Signs Major Contract." *San Jose Mercury News,* March 9, 2001.

Schlosser, Eric. "Strawberry Fields." *The Atlantic Monthly,* November 1995.

Steinbeck, John. *The Grapes of Wrath.* New York: Alfred A. Knopf, 1993.

Taylor, Ronald B. "Chavez's Union: A Future?" *The New York Times,* February 8, 1975.

Velie, Leslie. *Desperate Bargain: Why Jimmy Hoffa Had to Die.* Reader's Digest Press. New York: 1977.

"Grape Boycot Called Off." The Associated Press, November 22, 2000.

"The Little Strike that Grew to La Causa." *Time,* July 4, 1969.

Websites

A History of the Mexican-American People
http://www.jsri.msu.edu/museum/pubs/MexAmHist/

Cesar E. Chavez Institute for Public Policy
http://www.sfsu.edu/~cecipp/cesar_chavez/chavezhome.htm

The Democratic Promise: Saul Alinsky and His Legacy
http://www.itvs.org/democraticpromise/alinsky.html

The Fight in the Fields: Cesar Chavez and the Farmworkers Struggle
http://www.pbs.org/itvs/fightfields/

Surviving the Dust Storm
http://www.pbs.org/wgbh/amex/dustbowl/

Teamsters Union
http://www.teamster.org

United Farm Workers
http://www.ufw.org

Weedpatch Camp
http://www.weedpatchcamp.com

Further Reading

Brill, Steven. *The Teamsters.* New York: Simon and Schuster, 1978.

De Toledano, Ralph. *Little Cesar.* Washington: Anthem Books, 1971.

Dunne, John Gregory. *Delano: The Story of the California Grape Strike.* New York: Farrar, Straus and Giroux, 1967.

Ferriss, Susan, and Ricardo Sandoval. *The Fight in the Fields: Cesar Chavez and the Farmworkers Movement.* New York: Harcourt Brace and Company, 1997.

Galaraza, Ernesto. *Farm Workers and Agri-business in California, 1947-1960.* South Bend, Indiana: University of Notre Dame Press, 1977.

Matthiessen, Peter. *Sal Si Puedes: Cesar Chavez and the New American Revolution.* New York: Random House, 1969.

Steinbeck, John. *The Grapes of Wrath.* New York: Alfred A. Knopf, 1993.

Index

Picture Credits

About the Author

Hal Marcovitz is a journalist for The Morning Call, a newspaper based in Allentown, Pennsylvania. He has written more than 40 books for young readers. His other title in the Hispanics of Achievement series is a biography of Mexican revolutionary leader Pancho Villa. He makes his home in Chalfont, Pennsylvania, with his wife, Gail, and daughters Michelle and Ashley.